SKOOLIE!

SKOOLIE!

HOW TO CONVERT *a* SCHOOL BUS *or* VAN *into a* TINY HOME *or* RECREATIONAL VEHICLE

will sutherland

CREATOR OF WILLBILLYS

Storey Publishing

The mission of Storey Publishing is to serve our customers by publishing practical information that encourages personal independence in harmony with the environment.

EDITED BY CARLEEN MADIGAN

ART DIRECTION AND BOOK DESIGN BY CAROLYN ECKERT

TEXT PRODUCTION BY LISEANN KARANDISECKY

INDEXED BY NANCY D. WOOD

COVER PHOTOGRAPHY BY © ELI MEIR KAPLAN, front (t.c), spine, back (t.c. & b.c.); © **WILL SUTHERLAND**, front (t.l.) and back (t.r., b.r.); **CARLEEN MADIGAN**, front (t.r.); © **TRENT BELL PHOTOGRAPHY** for Winkelman Architecture, front (b.) and back (l.)

INTERIOR PHOTOGRAPHY BY © WILL SUTHERLAND, inside front cover, endpaper B and C, 1, 2 m.c., 5, 6 t.l., t.r., b.r, 7 t., 8–9, 12 r., 13 r., 14, 17 ex. b.c., 21, 23, 26 r., 27 t.l. & r., 29, 33–37, 39, 41 b., 42 b., 43 r.t. & r.b., 45–46, 52, 57 t.l., 60 l., 66–67, 72, 74, 75 m.r., 77 t. & b.r., 78, 79 r., 87 b.l. & r., 88, 89 t.l., 90, 92–95, 97, 101, 103 t.r., 106 b.r., 107, 110, 114 b., 115–117, 127, 129, 134–136, 139, 151 ex. t.l., 154–157, 158 l., 160 t.l., 161 r.t., 163, 166–167, 172–173, 178, 180–184, 185 b., 186 l., 187, 188 b., 189, 191, 193 m.l. & b., 194 t., 195, 198, 203;

© **ELI MEIR KAPLAN**, endpaper A, inside back cover, 2 b.c., 3, 6 t.c., m. (all), b.l. & c., 7 m. & b., 11, 15 l. & c., 17 b.c., 19, 25, 26 l., 27 b.l.., 28, 31, 40, 47, 53–56, 57 ex. t.l., 58–59, 60 r., 61–65, 73, 75 t.r., 77 b.l. & b.c., 79 l., 84–86, 87 t.l. & r., 89 ex. t. l., 91, 96, 99–100, 102, 103 ex. t.r., 104–105, 106 t. & b.l., 108–109, 111–113, 114 ex. b., 123, 128, 144, 147, 149, 151 t.l., 153, 158 r., 159, 160 ex. t.l., 161 l. & r.b., 164 l., 168–170, 171 b., 192, 193 t. & m.r., 194 b., 196, 199, 201–202, 207–208

ADDITIONAL INTERIOR PHOTOGRAPHY BY Courtesy of © Adventuringwithlola, 2 b.l., 48–51, 190; Courtesy of © Austin and Adrian Larsen, 165; Bethany Randall/Unsplash, 75 m.c., 204; © Betsy Johnson, Photographer, 2 b.r., 12 c., 15 r., 20, 41 t., 43 l., 122, 124, 126, 130–133, 164 r., 179, 197; © BusNBreakfast, 2 m.r., 13 c., 42 t., 75 t.l., 118–121; © carroteater/iStock.com, 16 l.; © Dean Chytraus, endpaper D, The Skoolie, 80–83; Elizabeth Lies/Unsplash, 75 b.c.; © Gilles_Paire/iStock.com, 185 t.; © Image Management/Alamy Stock Photo, 16 r.; © Matt Sloane/@campdavid.otr (owner)/@skoolie.homes (builder), 2 t.r., 12 l., 13 l., 68–71, 75 t.c., 145, 162; © Michael Fuehrer, Navigationnowhere, 75 b.r., 125; © Moon Safari/iStock.com, 27 b.r.; © One Wild Ride, 2 t.c., 44, 75 m.l., 137, 174–177; © RiverNorthPhotography/Getty Images, 24; Sharon Wright/Unsplash, 75 b.l.; © Stacie Jameson, Blue Ridge Conversions, 138; © Suzanne Tucker/Shutterstock.com, 18; Thomas Loizeau/Unsplash, 206; © Trent Bell Photography for Winkelman Architecture, 10, 38, 140, 142 t.l. & b.l., 143 l. & r.b.; Troy and Cindy Dickens @ whitewhaleskoolie, 186 r.t. & b., 188 t.l. & r.; Courtesy of William Winkelman, Winkelman Architecture, 2 t.l. & m.l., 141, 142 t.r. & b.r., 143 r.t.; Zachary Rorick, 171 t.

TEXT © 2019 BY WILL SUTHERLAND

STOREY PUBLISHING
210 MASS MoCA Way
North Adams, MA 01247
storey.com

Printed in China by Toppan Leefung Printing Ltd.
10 9 8 7 6 5 4 3 2 1

Library of Congress Cataloging-in-Publication Data

Names: Sutherland, Will (Donald Will), 1984– author.
Title: Skoolie! : how to convert a school bus or van into a tiny home or recreational vehicle / by Will Sutherland.
Description: North Adams, MA : Storey Publishing, [2019] | Includes index. | Identifiers: LCCN 2019011076 (print) | LCCN 2019021469 (ebook) | ISBN 9781635860733 (Ebook) | ISBN 9781635860726 (hardcover : alk. paper)
Subjects: LCSH: Small houses—Design and construction—Guidebooks. | Recreational vehicles—Design and construction—Guidebooks. | School Buses—Remodeling for other use—Guidebooks. | Owner-built houses—Design and construction—Guidebooks. | LCGFT: Guidebooks.
Classification: LCC NA7533 (ebook) | LCC NA7533 .S88 2019 (print) | DDC 728/.3—dc23
LC record available at https://lccn.loc.gov/2019011076

DEDICATION

THIS BOOK is for my mother, Jane Barkley Sutherland, who is my inspiration for everything creative. Her support and encouragement to think outside the box, be unique, and love life have been the foundation upon which I live my life. I hope this book will help others discover their creative side, just as my mother did for me and for countless students she had throughout her life. Thank you, Mom.

CONTENTS

PREFACE

I AM ONE OF THE MILLIONS OF young adults who entered adult life six weeks after college with a daunting amount of student loan debt. The idea of owning my own home seemed as distant a possibility as living on the moon. But as it turned out, the economic recession that caused the housing market to crash enabled me to purchase a small (900-square-foot) home. I traded in my newer truck for a less expensive car, took on a second job, and just barely qualified for the house.

After moving in and settling down in my traditional home, I began to dream of living more uniquely and less trapped by my bills. Despite the excitement of owning my own home, I still felt part of a rat race where I worked to afford a house that I didn't actually get to enjoy very often.

It was around this time that the tiny house craze was born, and I wanted one! I picked a spot on my property, drew out some designs, and went to work digging holes for foundation posts. I had the entire foundation complete and was ready to build the walls when disaster struck. A *derecho* (a powerful thunderstorm) devastated our area, an hour west of Washington, DC, bringing down eight giant trees on my property and ruining my tiny-house progress. By the time I had cleared all the downed trees, winter was upon us, yet my itch for tiny living hadn't faded. I started to think outside the box and looked at a few recreational vehicles, travel trailers, and even box trucks.

THEN, I FOUND A SCHOOL BUS.

My friends thought I was nuts, but I had an overwhelming feeling in my gut that making a tiny house out of a school bus was meant to be. My first bus was a crash course of trial and error. Meanwhile, through social media, I was making new friends who were converting buses as well, and together we came up with all sorts of ideas and solutions. My first skoolie was an escape from the textbook American dream of going to college, getting a job, and buying a home.

With this book, I want readers to feel hopeful that there are other routes to successful, joyful lives that allow for more travel and outdoor adventures, all while having a smaller impact on the environment. I hope you'll use this book as a base for envisioning and creating your *own* American dream!

SCHOOL *why a* BUS?

①

Regardless of how large or small your budget is, how many windows your bus has, how elaborate your interior is, or how large your solar array may be, you will undoubtedly enjoy your skoolie. It promises an adventurous life in a comfortable home that's also a reliable vehicle.

living the SKOOLIE LIFE

HOW CAN I begin to explain how exciting and inspiring it is to own your own home that is unlike any other? A home that can be relocated with ease while maintaining a comfortable setup with just a small carbon footprint? Tiny living opens up an entire new perspective on the American dream, whether it's in an RV, tiny house, van, or skoolie. I grew up in a time where "living in a van down by the river" was laughed at, but now that idea actually sounds like a great life!

LIFESTYLE CHANGES that come with owning a skoolie are abundant, such as not having to pay for a motel room if you decide to venture out for a weekend. And while tent camping is great, it's not something you can do year-round. Living in a skoolie will force you to be outdoors more often, adapting to the weather, getting plenty of vitamin D from the sunshine, and just living a more active life overall.

EVENTS that will make your skoolie shine range from music festivals to family gatherings. Anytime you have an overnight adventure planned, your skoolie awaits! Be prepared for lots of attention at festivals; everyone will be jealous of your setup. Being able to stay in my own skoolie during family reunions is one of my favorite benefits.

ENTERTAINMENT on board your skoolie can be as simple as a deck of cards or as complex as a projector screen and surround-sound system. A laptop or tablet with an Internet connection is all you really need for those rainy days, but there are fancier options. Flat-screen TVs are lightweight and energy efficient, and pico projectors can connect to your smartphone and provide a large screen. You can literally have a wall-size image in your bus for a few hundred bucks or less.

MAKE MONEY from your skoolie when you're not using it! The community of people who use Airbnb and other travel accommodation apps are on the prowl for unique places to stay. If you allow paying guests on your bus for two weekends out of the month, you could easily cover a couple monthly bills.

PEOPLE YOU MEET in the skoolie community are some of the most genuine folks you will ever encounter. Being a part of that community alone is worth the effort of building a skoolie. Instagram is a great place to connect, share ideas, and solve problems with other skoolie owners. Be warned: you will have to get used to doing impromptu "bus tours" for curious people you meet on your travels. You might be amazed at how many folks are intrigued by a skoolie.

why A SCHOOL BUS MAKES A GREAT HOME

WHEN YOU THINK of a school bus, you might not consider it as a potential dwelling. That's understandable. We are familiar with pull-behind campers, motor homes, conversion vans, and tiny houses, so why consider a bus instead? There are four very good reasons.

OWNING A SKOOLIE IS A WONDERFUL LIFESTYLE. It gives you the freedom to roam. "Home is where you park it" is just one phrase that summarizes life in a skoolie. Unlike most dwellings, your skoolie will be unique and customized to your needs and preferences. When you embark on a road trip and

reach your destination, your home will always stand out rather than blending in, making it feel even more special. Also, you will make skoolie friends! When you meet a fellow skoolie owner, there is a connection like no other. You will speak the same skoolie language, share the same experiences, and, most important, have a similar view of how to live alternatively.

A SCHOOL BUS IS EXTREMELY DURABLE.

A vehicle designed to transport 72 young lives is built with safety and sturdiness in mind. School buses are constructed on heavy-duty commercial truck frames by bus manufacturers such as Blue Bird and Thomas. The school bus body itself is framed with steel tubing and covered with steel paneling. On the exterior, there are additional thin sections of corrugated steel: known as rub rails, these are designed to minimize body damage from sideswiping and add to the structural integrity of the bus.

On top of a school bus, you will find a steel-framed, rounded metal roof designed to withstand extreme pressure from a rollover accident. Inside, light-gauge steel panels on the walls and ceiling are most commonly attached with rivets, but sometimes (especially in older buses) they are attached with regular screws. Under the hood, nearly all school buses feature diesel engines, which are known for their commercial-grade durability and power. Needless to say, a school bus is built tough!

By contrast, regular campers and RVs are constructed with affordability and weight in mind. A quick Internet search of "RV accidents" will give you an idea of what happens

to them in a wreck. RVs are largely constructed with lightweight wood and fiberglass for the walls and roof. The roofs are flat, making them prone to water damage if they are not sealed and kept under cover regularly.

Tiny homes are solidly built and typically feature the same materials and construction as regular-size homes, but they are designed more for a permanent location rather than frequent travel. Tiny homes typically are mounted on trailers as a way to avoid building code restrictions and to make them technically movable (as in nonpermanent dwellings). They're not really designed to be routinely out and about on the highway.

SCHOOL BUSES ARE WELL MAINTAINED.
School systems maintain their buses as a fleet. The phrase "fleet maintained" seen in ad listings is a good thing! Each bus gets routine oil changes and thorough inspections, and repair and maintenance costs are prebudgeted, so issues are quickly taken care of. By contrast, if you're shopping for an affordable used RV, it's possible the previous owner neglected to repair an issue in a timely fashion, which could lead to more wear and tear on other parts as well as a compromised overall mechanical function — problems you will have to face as the new owner.

SCHOOL BUSES ARE AFFORDABLE.
Most school systems retire some buses each year based on age or mileage. I have found that most buses are kept in service for up to 10 years or 250,000 miles. Retired buses are usually auctioned off or sold in bulk to a dealer. A typical school bus may be auctioned for roughly a tenth of the cost of a used motor home or a tiny house.

Used RVs and tiny homes simply cannot compete with the value of a used school bus. Sure, there are many happy folks traveling in traditional motor homes and sleeping in trendy tiny homes, but maybe you don't have that kind of budget, and maybe you want to go enjoy your life and independence sooner rather than later.

In addition, skoolies are simply cool! Skoolie owners soak up frequent thumbs-ups and peace signs from other drivers and enjoy giving the inquisitive couple at every stop a glimpse into their creative, unique, and liberating skoolie lifestyle.

BUS HUNTING 101

CHOOSING AND ACQUIRING A SOON-TO-BE SKOOLIE!

There are several priorities to take into consideration when choosing the right bus for your skoolie transformation. Square footage is obviously a main priority, but what about maneuverability and your planned usage? Start by deciding what your bus will be used for and choosing an appropriate type and size. Then, it's time to shop around and buy your first bus!

A full-size school bus can be up to 40 feet in length, with nearly 300 square feet of interior space.

which SCHOOL BUS IS FOR ME?

THE BEST SIZE of bus depends on what you need. School buses come in three basic sizes: short, midsize, and full-size. A short bus offers the maneuverability of a van along with enough headroom to stand upright inside (which you can't do in most vans). Short buses are popular for weekend travelers and those who prefer a minimal amount of living space — a lot of people living in short buses spend the majority of their time outside, whether they're rafting, climbing, or skiing. Midsize buses offer a good blend of drivability and square footage. Plenty of couples live happily in their midsize buses year-round without compromising too much legroom. Full-size buses are for those who want to live full time in their skoolies with enough space for all of the elements of a home plus space for kids or a lot of pets!

Sizing Up a School Bus

An easy way to roughly estimate the interior space of a bus is to count the number of passenger windows on one side and make a quick calculation. A full-size bus typically has 12 or more windows, a midsize bus has 6 to 11 windows, and a short bus has 4 to 6 windows. I have seen 3-window buses, but they're more like a van than a bus.

Estimate each window to be 30 inches wide, including the window pillars. This means an 8-window bus is roughly 20 feet long inside (30 inches × 8 windows, divided by 12 inches = 20 feet). Most buses are 7½ feet wide inside, so multiplying the length in feet by 7.5 will give you the square footage of livable space. So, an 8-window bus will be roughly 150 square feet inside, and a 12-window bus will be around 225 square feet. By comparison, a typical tiny house is between 100 and 400 square feet.

FULL-SIZE BUSES

Full-size buses are the norm for most folks who live in their skoolies full-time, but this also depends on the size of their household or family. If you have youngsters, you'll want to accommodate bunk beds. If you're planning to work from home, you may need space for an office. If you have three dogs, you may want a designated area for them. There are tons of different scenarios, so think hard about what would work best for you.

Inevitably, when you first sit down in the driver's seat of a full-size school bus, you will be intimidated by the vehicle's size. The steering wheel is nearly twice the diameter of those on cars, and the seat is more than a foot away from the driver's side of the bus, making it harder to visualize the overall width.

When driving a full-size bus, you need to pay close attention to the various mirrors that help you make turns and keep the bus centered in the lane. Also, buses take more time to get up to speed and to stop, so keep that in mind when turning onto roads or approaching a stop sign or red light. Fortunately, driving a school bus is something you'll pick up quickly and even grow to enjoy. Just remember to keep both hands on the wheel and both eyes on the road!

MIDSIZE BUSES

The midsize bus, also known as a three-quarters bus, is my favorite size. It's easier to park and maneuver on tight roads than a full-size, and it still has a decent amount of interior space. Unfortunately, midsize buses are less common than full-size because they're not in as much demand by school districts. Wheelchair-accessible buses are often midsize or short

Midsize school buses offer the perfect balance of good maneuverability and a livable amount of interior space.

buses and usually don't have as many miles as a full-size due to shorter daily routes.

If you find a wheelchair-accessible bus and you don't need the chair lift, you can remove the lift to create a nice, wide side door that could be very useful, depending on your interior layout.

Midsize buses share some of the same driving characteristics of a full-size bus, but they make turns more easily and don't require as much space to turn around. Sometimes you can find a midsize bus that has a dedicated driver's door, similar to short buses, but this feature is rare.

SHORT BUSES

Short buses are perfect for many people. A lot of van-life folks make the bold move from a van to a short bus because the pros greatly outweigh the cons. Short buses are typically just a couple feet longer than a van but up to 1½ feet wider. The biggest advantage over a van is that you can stand up in a bus. All van lifers would love to be able to stand upright in their vehicles, which is why the taller Sprinter vans have become popular. Unfortunately, Sprinter vans are not as wide as a short school bus — and definitely not as affordable!

A short bus is the least challenging of all school buses to drive. A short bus is built on a van chassis rather than a large truck chassis. Unlike larger buses, most short buses have a driver's-side door, which makes getting in and out of the bus easier and gives the driver a more conventional feel when maneuvering the bus.

Most short buses are the same width as a full-size bus (7½ feet), so the driver still needs to keep the extra width in mind when making turns and staying centered on the road. Although the overall height of a short bus is less than that of midsize and full-size buses, short buses still need more clearance than a van.

FLAT-FRONT BUSES

Flat-front buses are almost as common as full-size buses. A flat-front bus, also known as a flat-nose bus, is typically found in a full-size configuration with as many as 15 passenger windows! It is often assumed that a flat-front bus's engine is in the rear, making it a "pusher" style of bus (because the engine is pushing from the rear rather than pulling from the front). In reality, many flat-front school buses site the engine in the front, tucked below the driver's area. Midsize flat-front buses do exist, but they aren't as common as full-size. Compared to a conventional bus, a flat-nose bus with the engine in the front generates more interior noise when you're driving, but all school buses are relatively noisy compared to a car.

Driving a flat-nose bus is unique in that the driver sits above or slightly in front of the front tires, which maximizes visibility when turning the bus. This benefit aside, the same learning curve that applies to regular buses also applies to operating a flat-front bus.

Note Your CLEARANCE

Buses — including short buses — need more clearance than cars or RVs to get safely under bridges and down back roads (watch out for tree branches!). Measure the overall height of the bus (including things like roof vents or decks) so you know how much overhead clearance it needs. Post the minimum clearance dimension (10 feet, 12 feet, and so on) inside the bus so the number is clearly visible from the driver's seat. When you're barreling down the highway and see a road sign that says CLEARANCE 12' 6", you don't want to be trying to remember how tall your bus is (or asking the owner, if it's not your bus).

Most flat-front buses are full size and provide the greatest amount of interior space. They also have improved visibility from the front seat, because the driver's seat is ahead of the front wheels.

Where to BUY A SKOOLIE

ONCE YOU'VE DECIDED to buy a bus, it is understandably an exciting time, but it is *very* important to be patient and hunt for the right vehicle! Finding a bus for your skoolie conversion can be done in several ways. The most common way is through online listings, such as Craigslist. Oftentimes buses listed online were purchased in bulk at auctions and are being resold individually, but there are also private sellers of individual buses.

Bus Auctions

Most school districts auction off their buses, and the vehicles are often bought in bulk by individuals who resell them for a profit. These auctions usually take place near the end of the academic year and are commonly under-advertised or heard about only through word of mouth. One way to find out where buses will be auctioned is by contacting local school bus garages and simply asking.

When bidding for a bus at an auction, you may have to compete with bidders who buy five or more buses at a time, which usually means they won't pay a lot for each bus. You will simply have to offer slightly more money than these buyers to win the bidding.

Before bidding, conduct a detailed inspection (see pages 25–30) of the bus and ask for any service records, or ask to speak with one of the mechanics familiar with the vehicle. Typically, buses at auctions can be inspected only while parked; they cannot be test-driven.

In recent years, many school districts have begun selling retired buses via online auction sites because they can tap a larger market and make more money. On auction sites, you can browse buses from all over the country and place bids. After winning a bid, you typically get a week to pick up the bus. If you're bidding long-distance, you'll have to assume the risks of a sight-unseen purchase (that is, no inspection or test-drive). If the bus is within reasonable driving distance, you should make the effort to inspect it before battling for the winning bid.

Private Sales

Private bus sales aren't uncommon! Many groups and organizations that use buses, such as churches, private schools, and river guide outfitters, occasionally need to replace their vehicles with newer models. What's nice about a private sale is that you can negotiate some on the price, and you can usually get a lot of information about the bus from a long-term owner. I like to keep a close watch for listings on several websites — such as Craigslist, the Facebook marketplace, and Letgo — as well as online and in print newspaper classifieds, because you never know what might pop up.

Buying a bus from a private organization, such as a church or an outdoor outfitter, is a good option, especially if there isn't a bus auction near you.

Inspect a bus thoroughly before buying it. Don't be afraid to get underneath it and poke around with a screwdriver to see how much rust comes off.

INSPECTING YOUR BUS
before BUYING

ALTHOUGH SOME SKOOLIE folks assume the risks of buying a bus sight unseen, I believe that inspecting a bus before handing over the payment is a must! Once you have decided on the type of bus you want and have located a vehicle, measure it to be sure it's the right size. Then, it's time for a thorough inspection to ensure the bus will make a good skoolie platform. Be patient!

Rust

Rust is a major factor to consider when selecting a bus and is especially common on buses in areas of the country that see a lot of snow. Over time, road salt causes metal to rust unless it is carefully washed off after the bus is exposed. Many folks like to hunt for buses in warmer climates to avoid rust issues.

Salespeople can be tricky in disguising rust! Be on the lookout for freshly painted spots on the body or the frame rails that may be hiding rust. Also, be wary of listings that have no undercarriage photos. In any case, a careful inspection will uncover the truth. There are several hot spots I check on a bus to get an indication of the overall presence of rust. First, any obvious body rust is a red flag and essentially a deal breaker: if I find it, I won't bother inspecting the bus further. If the body appears rust-free, I continue to check for rust in the following key areas.

UNDERNEATH THE BUS. Some surface rust on the frame and body-frame supports is common, but the underside of the bus floor should be free of any rust. It's a no-go if the primary frame rails that run the length of the bus have rust that flakes off in your hand. Rust that flakes from bus body-frame supports that span the width of the bus is less serious if only a couple rails show rust flaking, because these rails can be treated with rust remover, but it is a definite no-go if most of the body support rails have flaking rust. Also check for rusty brake and fuel lines, which are usually tucked inside the frame rails. Check carefully underneath the stairwell: often, bus passenger doors aren't shut tight when the bus is parked, allowing rainwater to get in and create rust.

EMERGENCY DOOR. Check the area around the back emergency door, mainly

Inspect the frame rails and underside of the bus body for rust. Although surface rust is common, rust holes are a bad sign. Underneath the rubber flooring, next to the stairwell (above, right), is a common place for rust to occur. You can't start pulling up the floor before you buy the bus, but you can feel for soft spots.

around the sill. Open the emergency door and inspect for rust around the front of the sill and also along the bottom of the back wall of the bus.

BODY. Look for small rust spots on the exterior of the bus that are at the height of the floor; these indicate that rust is coming from the inside and migrating out. You can test for soft spots in the body simply by pressing against the body with your thumb or knocking with a light object such as the handle of a screwdriver. You can also use a magnet to check for body repairs made with fiberglass body filler; if the magnet doesn't stick, the material isn't metal (although it could be aluminum, which is not magnetic).

FLOOR. Inside the bus, walk between all the seats and check for softness in the floor, which indicates rot in the wood. Search around the "wheel humps" for rust, and pay attention to the area where the wall meets the floor. Although you can check for the majority of rust issues before buying a bus, there may be rust lurking under the floor that will be visible only after the demolition process. I will explain how to tackle floor rust in chapter 6.

Tires

Tires are another important item to inspect before purchasing a bus. Bus tires are similar to semi truck tires and can last more than 100,000 miles, but the tire tread itself is not the only point of inspection. Dry-rotted tires are just as dangerous as a bald tire. Even if a tire appears to have excellent tread, if you see cracking or rubber pieces peeling off or missing in the sidewall, it is likely the tire is old and in need of replacement.

Tires have their manufacture date stamped on the sidewall near the "DOT" (see opposite page) code. The first two numbers indicate the week, and the next two numbers the year. Typically, tires over 10 years old should be replaced.

When you drive on dry-rotted or bald tires, you are putting yourself and other drivers at risk. A bus tire is much heavier than a car tire; if it blows out on the road, it can cause a lot of damage.

Be aware that a bus that has sat unused for a long time may develop flat spots in its tires, which can cause a bumpy ride and inconsistent handling. During a test-drive, these flat spots result in a small bounce for every tire rotation, increasing in frequency as you go faster. If the tires aren't outdated, the flat spots will likely work themselves out.

Fortunately, most bus garages are vigilant about keeping their bus tires safe and sound. But if you have found the perfect bus and its only flaws are its tires, then by all means don't be afraid to invest in a new set. Although new bus tires are costly, the peace of mind you get from knowing you have a new, well-balanced set of tires that will last you for years is worth the investment.

Tire SCHOOL

The rear tires on buses are known as drive tires and the front ones are referred to as steer tires because they have different tread designs specifically for steering and drive traction. Bus tire tread can be measured just like a typical car tire, by measuring the depth of the tread with a ruler, coin, or tire tread depth gauge. There are businesses that specialize in commercial truck tire sales, and you can drive your bus right to their shop to get the tires replaced, just as you would with a car. Tires are included in the inspection process (after the bus is registered and insured and ready to get an inspection sticker). The inspector will look for damaged tires as well as poor tread, but it's also important to inspect tires regularly on your own.

The front tires (left) on a school bus are known as the "steer tires" and have a much different tread pattern than the rear tires (right), which are the "drive tires."

The DOT stamp indicates how old a tire is; it shows the week and year the tire was manufactured (in this case, 0602, or the sixth week of 2002).

Inspect your tires carefully, to be sure they have a reasonable amount of tread left on them; bald tires like this one will need to be replaced.

Engine

Engine mileage is one of the first details you see in bus listings. A bus used regularly for a decade can log more than 200,000 miles, which sounds intimidating to most of us, but it also means that the engine probably was serviced well. A properly-cared-for bus engine can last at least 300,000 miles.

TYPES OF BUS ENGINES

Most full-size and midsize buses currently in use will have one of four engines:

- Navistar DT466
- Navistar T444E
- Cummins 5.9L
- Caterpillar 3126

Older full and medium buses can be found with Detroit Diesels, big- and small-block Chevrolet gasoline (not diesel) engines, and occasionally something less common, depending on the age of the bus.

Generally speaking, the DT466 engine is considered the best because it is rated for more weight than the average school bus can carry, and it has the potential to be rebuilt without removing the engine from the bus. There are millions of DT466 engines on the road.

The T444E engine also is common, but a full-size bus is nearing the maximum amount that engine is rated to haul. The Cummins 5.9L engine is a favorite for many people and similar to the T444E in power output. The Caterpillar engine is well liked by many bus owners, but its repair costs are usually higher. Note that the T444E engine often is referred to as a "7.3 diesel" or "Power Stroke diesel," but it is far from identical to the 7.3 Power Stroke engines found in older Ford trucks.

Some of the latest buses have Mercedes engines, which come with higher repair costs than those of the more common DT466 and T444E motors. Mercedes commercial diesel engines are much less common in the United States, but in Europe they have a good reputation for reliability and emissions.

Short buses usually have a Chevrolet 6.2, 6.5 nonturbo, or 6.5 turbo, or a Ford 7.3 Power Stroke (same as the older Ford trucks) or 6.0 turbo diesel. As with the larger full-size bus engines, the smaller diesel engines have good potential to last 300,000 or more miles when properly maintained, but older Ford 6.0 turbo engines require extensive preventive upgrades, commonly referred to as "bulletproofing," to keep high-mileage issues in check.

ENGINE INSPECTION

Always ask for any available maintenance documentation for the bus. If you have a mechanic or friends who know their way around a diesel engine, bring one of them along to inspect the engine with you.

Plan to start up the bus and let the engine run to check the batteries and gauges. When you turn the key partway, you'll usually see a brief alert on the dash telling you to "wait to start." This is standard for diesel engines and allows time for the glow plugs to heat up sufficiently to start the engine. When the alert light goes off, turn the key all the way to start the engine; it should turn over quickly. Some newer engines do not have this "wait to start" light (due to technological advancements), but be sure to check prior to fully turning the key.

If the engine isn't turning over quickly, there may be an issue with the batteries. Diesel engines require a lot of cranking-amps to start, so they usually have two batteries. If a bus for-sale listing includes "just needs batteries," be prepared to spend a few hundred dollars on new ones. The batteries need to be able to start the bus without hesitation during your initial inspection process as well.

Once the bus is running, it will seem sluggish until the engine warms up (especially in the winter) and the oil in the engine becomes less thick. The engine should get up to the normal operating temperature on the gauge. If the gauge goes into the red section at any time, the engine is overheating and can be damaged quickly. (This is why it's *always* important to keep a watch on the temperature gauge in case there's a sudden coolant leak or heat from the engine overwhelms the cooling

(Left) Buses typically have very durable, commercial diesel engines that get around 10 miles per gallon. Transmission models can be identified by the model number stamped on a metal tag or cast into the transmission case.

(Right) Check for spots that appear wet around the engine, transmission, and rear axle; a wet area could indicate a leak.

system during a long hill climb.) The oil pressure gauge will read high when the motor is cold but will level off to a medium gauge reading after it's warm. The engine shouldn't smoke much, if at all, except for cold starts where a couple minutes of white smoke is normal. Some black smoke during hard acceleration also is normal.

Once you've confirmed normal readings on the gauges, you can now shut the engine off and check for signs of fluid leaks, including:

- Spots under the bus
- Oil spots on the frame
- Signs of dripping on the engine itself
- Coolant residue on the radiator
- Axle seal leaks on the insides of the wheels

Leaks may also be evident around the rear axle differential or "pumpkin" located in the center of the rear axle. Ideally, you will get to inspect the ground where the bus has been parked for at least a few days so that spots of fluid on the ground can alert you to areas to check for leaks.

In the long run, a well-cared-for bus engine probably will outlast the body of the bus, but it is wise to start a repair fund to handle unexpected costs. Always keep track of regular maintenance items, such as oil-change intervals and filter changes. If you need a mechanic, reach out to a local business that uses buses or commercial trucks and ask for recommendations. Getting several references for a trusted bus mechanic is important.

Transmission

Most buses have automatic transmissions. To identify what type of transmission a bus has, look for a small metal tag on the side of the transmission. Many bus classifieds advertise that a bus has "a highly-sought-after Allison transmission," which is a major selling point to anyone familiar with the reliability of an Allison — but don't get too excited yet.

While Allison transmissions are quite stout, some models, mainly the AT545, are considered underrated for the power the DT466 engine puts out. A T444E engine is evenly matched with the AT545 automatic, as are the Cummins 5.9L and Caterpillar engines. The DT466 is much better off with an Allison MT643 or MD3060 transmission. These models can handle the extra torque of the DT466 because their torque converters fully lock with the engine in fourth gear rather than allowing slippage, which creates heat. Excessive heat is a big threat for any transmission.

Manual transmissions are seldom seen in buses, but they do exist, and they are plenty strong, reliable, and well suited for all engine sizes. They are less complex than an automatic, and they don't generate as much heat because the gears do not allow for any slippage during torque conversion. Operating a manual transmission in a bus is much like what you're used to in any manual-transmission car, only the gear shifter has more travel and you won't be shifting it like you do a sports car! Personally, I love manual-transmission buses because of their simplicity. I always know what gear I'm in, there are fewer moving parts to malfunction, they don't generate as much internal heat, and I enjoy shifting through the gears.

Short buses typically have the same transmissions used in Ford or Chevrolet full-size trucks, and overall they are well suited for their engines.

In any case, the most important factor is how well the bus is cared for. You shouldn't let a transmission-and-engine combination alone rule out a bus that is a good fit for you. If a transmission disaster does strike, a used Allison AT545 transmission can be purchased relatively inexpensively.

Brakes

Bus brakes are either hydraulic (similar to your car) or air powered. Hydraulic brakes work by applying pressure to fluid traveling through brake lines to the brakes themselves. When the brake pedal is released by the driver, the brakes back away from the brake drums or discs. Air brakes work in the opposite direction. They use pressurized air to hold the brake calipers and pads off the drums or discs when the brakes are not being applied by the driver. If there is a leak in the air supply, the brakes will apply themselves instead of leaving the bus careening out of control.

Air brakes are considered more powerful than hydraulic brakes and are preferred for larger buses due to their added stopping power, but they are also less conventional and therefore more expensive to have repaired. Air brakes have a compressor that fills a reservoir tank with air for the braking system, which creates that startling *pshhhh* sound you hear from large vehicles. Regardless of brake style, buses have very large braking systems that are designed to stop the full carrying capacity of the bus chassis, and they are durable and resistant to wear.

For hydraulic brakes, check the brake fluid container under the hood to be sure it's full. For air brakes, there may be an indicator light on the dash that illuminates when air pressure is low, or there will be an audible alarm indicating low air pressure or an air leak. The absence of a dash light or alarm means your air brake system is functioning properly. That said, it is important to test the brakes before getting out on the road to test-drive a bus!

Test-Driving A SCHOOL BUS

TEST-DRIVING IS POSSIBLY the biggest step in inspecting a bus. After you have inspected for rust, evaluated the tires, identified the engine and transmission types, and checked fluid levels, it's time to take the bus for a spin!

The first thing you will notice is that buses are big! You will inevitably feel intimidated during your maiden voyage as captain of a bus. Just relax, remember to be patient, and follow the basic startup procedure:

The first time behind the wheel of a bus can be very intimidating. Be sure to check the mirrors frequently while driving — especially when making turns.

1. Position the driver's seat to your liking and adjust the mirrors to maximize your view.

2. Fasten the seat belt.

3. Turn the key partially to activate the "wait to start" or glow-plug indicator light. Once this light goes off, crank the bus.

4. Let the bus run for a couple minutes to warm up. Use this time to check the gauges to make sure you have readings, then check signal lights and the horn. The engine will smooth out once the oil has warmed, and you'll be ready to take a spin.

5. Release the parking brake. If the bus has air brakes, there will be a brake pressure valve located on the dash; if it has hydraulic brakes, there will be a traditional parking brake pedal or lever.

6. Put the bus in drive, let it inch forward some, then test the brake pressure. Buses with air brakes don't always have a "P" for park on the transmission selector because the air brakes themselves act as "park" when the air brake parking valve is on. You can use "N" for neutral instead of leaving the bus in drive when parked. Once you're in drive, make sure the brake pedal doesn't go to the floor. If it does, immediately reengage the parking brake, put the bus in park (or neutral with air brakes), and alert the seller to the brake failure. If the brakes feel solid and seem to function properly, continue with your test-drive.

Driving behaviors for a good-condition bus should be obvious. The brakes will be strong and even, with no left or right pull and no vibration in the brake pedal or steering wheel. Steering will be tight, with minimal play in the wheel, and the suspension should be firm rather than bouncy or "leaning" when making turns. Acceleration will be slow but should be steady. The transmission should shift smoothly and quickly, and you shouldn't feel any unusual vibrations or "thumps" during gear changes. It's possible the tires will have some flat spots from the bus sitting for a while, but these should round out after a few minutes.

Test-drive the bus in a parking lot or on a slow back road at first to get a feel for how it drives. Once you're confident it can handle slower speeds, drive to a road that allows you to check the speed capability of the bus, and get it up to its governed speed. Keep in mind that school buses are not fast! Many buses are governed electronically or mechanically to limit their maximum speed to 55 to 65 mph. If the bus will do 60 mph, that's good news. If it will do 65 mph, even better!

Owning a skoolie is all about enjoying the journey, both physically and metaphorically, so remember to practice patience when driving. Once you have the bus up to its top speed, or the maximum speed allowed for the road you're testing it on, take note of the rpm on the tachometer; this tells you how fast the engine is turning. The higher the rpm, the lower the fuel economy. It's common for school buses to average up to 2,600 rpm at their maximum operating speed, but the ideal range is closer to 2,000 rpm. If the bus is screaming along at close to 3,000 rpm, it may indicate the transmission isn't shifting into its highest gear.

Once you've completed a test-drive of the bus and deemed it satisfactory, you can consider it for purchase. Keep in mind that the overall condition of a bus is important because it reflects how well it was cared for. A bus that has dents, broken windows, or excessive vibrations or rattles when driving is likely overused and undermaintained.

Do I Need A SPECIAL DRIVER'S LICENSE?

School bus drivers are required to have a CDL class B license to drive a bus that can carry more than 15 passengers. Also, the gross vehicle weight rating, or GVWR, dictates what type of license is required for a commercial vehicle. The GVWR is usually listed over the driver's seat on a decal, or you can refer to the vehicle title.

In most states, commercial vehicles with a GVWR in excess of 26,000 pounds require a CDL, but if you are able to have your bus registered as an RV without the commercial vehicle rating, you will not need a CDL. Getting a CDL license is similar to getting a standard driver's license, but it requires attending a CDL driving school for training. These schools are easy to find through an online search, and you can also find videos online to help you prepare. Many skoolie drivers do not have CDL licenses because their buses are under the GVWR rating or because they have registered the bus as an RV.

Regardless of which license you get, it is crucial to exercise added caution and awareness of the bus size when behind the wheel. When making a tight turn, you will have to drive farther ahead than you would in a normal car in order to make the turn without side-swiping anything on the inside of the turn, all while keeping watch on the vehicles around you. (Think of a semi-truck initially going straight into an intersection then making a wide, sweeping turn; this is to get the back end through the turn without clipping the corner.)

Condition yourself to using the various bus mirrors to ensure you're clear of obstacles without looking over your shoulder, and watch for tree limbs and street signs that can stick out into the pathway of your bus.

Taking YOUR BUS HOME

YOU CAN'T DRIVE your new bus home until it is insured and has new license plates and registration. The insuring process is one of the most common questions asked about skoolies. I strongly suggest using an independent insurance agent, also known as an insurance broker. An independent agent will find insurance policies within a large network of insurance providers for a relatively small fee, or often for no fee at all. The same agents that provide insurance policies for the average car can find policy options for your bus.

Independent insurance agents also are helpful for working around VIN number databases, which tend to categorize vehicles too broadly. For example, if you were to call an insurance company directly, they would ask for the VIN number of the vehicle and see that it is a commercial VIN for a school bus, which requires a costlier commercial insurance policy. Insurance brokers can generate a policy with your bus listed as an RV or just as a large truck. Be sure to get several insurance quotes — you'll be surprised by how different they can be.

Once insured, you will be able to register your bus and get a license plate from the local department of motor vehicles (the good ol' DMV!). The exact process for registering your soon-to-be skoolie differs depending on what state you are located in. A bus's title will typically list only the chassis manufacturer model, such as "International 3800 series." The total gross vehicle weight rating (GVWR) of your bus will be listed over the driver's seat or on the title itself. This number specifies the maximum total weight the bus can weigh, including cargo, and it is sometimes referenced by the DMV to determine how large the vehicle is.

When you're dealing with the DMV, there is no need to describe your bus in any more detail than what the title reads. If you say "school bus," things can get a lot more complicated! Generally, unless you plan to leave the seats in your bus, it doesn't qualify as a passenger bus at all. Some states will ask for more detail of the vehicle model, especially if it's over a certain weight. Depending on the state, you may have to take your bus to a state inspector for legal proof the vehicle is no longer a school bus. If you want to register the vehicle as a recreational vehicle, you likely will have to go through the state inspection process. Again, registering varies from state to state, but it is typically an easy process. If you have an RV insurance policy, the DMV will require only the policy number, the insurance agent or company, and the National Association of Insurance Commissioner's number (known as the NAIC). You will not have to register the bus as an RV based on the insurance policy.

Taking your bus home is a wonderful feeling! Be sure you have a good spot to park your bus for the duration of the conversion process. If you live in a neighborhood with an HOA or covenant restrictions, be sure to deal with those in advance so you won't be forced to move your bus and stall your conversion process. I recommend parking in a level spot close to power outlets. Also, parking your bus where you will see it frequently will help motivate you to work on it!

Park your new bus wherever you'll have easy access while you're converting it.

BEHIND THE SCENES
OUR BOOK BUS

TO SHOW HOW TO RENOVATE A BUS FOR THIS BOOK, Sabrina and I actually purchased a bus and photographed the entire process. It affectionately became known as the "Book Bus." I found it on an online auction site and — after carefully inspecting the photos from the listing and speaking with the seller (who worked for a bus garage) — I purchased it. My Dad and I drove six hours to pick it up, and I drove it home . . . with no heat, in the middle of winter. That was an adventure! (As it turned out, a valve for the bus heater was turned off, but I didn't discover this until the bus was home.)

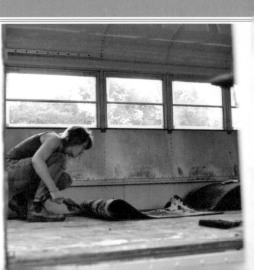

The process photos and finished shots throughout the book show the work we did on the bus. There are so many options when you're renovating a bus — from bare bones to super pricey — and we wanted to show a renovation that most people with basic skills could do themselves on a limited budget. For information on how much we spent to build the bus, turn to page 200.

3 LAYOUT and DESIGN

Although you may already have an idea of how you want your skoolie set up, those plans may change when you get your bus home and take precise measurements of the interior. Start by getting a sense of how much space you really have to work with, then map out a rough floor plan. You can refine your plans later when you get down to the nitty-gritty details of framing and finishing the interior spaces.

Measuring and Drawing the USABLE SPACE

FIRST, TAKE EXACT measurements of your bus's interior, then make a scaled drawing of it. Start with the following measurements:

- Distance between the walls
- Distance from the back of the driver's seat to the back of the bus
- Distance behind and in front of the wheel humps, from both ends of the bus
- Space between the wheel humps, from side to side
- Height from the middle (high point) of the ceiling to the floor

Next, create a scaled drawing on a piece of poster board or large sheet of paper. Use a ruler (and a square, if you have one) for accuracy, and scale the drawing so that 1 inch equals 1 foot. For example, if an area measures 20 feet on your bus, it will measure 20 inches on your drawing. You can use a smaller scale, such as ½ inch equals 1 foot, if you don't have a large piece of poster board or paper.

You can also brainstorm with small drawings on graph paper, then transfer the best ideas to a larger-scale drawing.

Bus interiors are roughly 7½ feet wide before insulation is added.

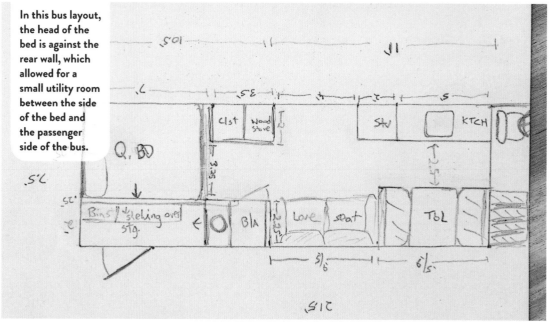

In this bus layout, the head of the bed is against the rear wall, which allowed for a small utility room between the side of the bed and the passenger side of the bus.

Carving Up THE SPACE

BEGIN BUILDING YOUR layout by prioritizing the things you value most for your skoolie conversion. Do you want a full-size bed, or would you rather allow more space for the kitchen or bathroom? What kind of furniture or built-ins would you like? What's your ideal kitchen layout? We'll discuss different options for all these interior fixtures in a moment, but for now, understand that having the dimensions of your bed, table, kitchen cabinets, and woodstove (and space around the woodstove), as well as any storage areas and walled-off areas, is crucial to ensuring that the final layout will work with the space you have.

Once you've determined the size of the interior fixtures, you'll create scale cutouts of anything that will take up space and be stationary. This makes it easy to rearrange them on the scaled bus drawing; you can experiment with layouts rather than drawing everything over again for each concept. Alternatively, if you have access to and experience using computer-aided design software (or even SketchUp), you can design your layouts digitally.

Bed

Do you need a queen-size bed, or are you okay with a double? A queen mattress is approximately 5 feet wide and 6½ feet long, but a double mattress is 4½ feet wide and just over 6 feet long. Half a foot of width could make or break your layout plans — or sleeping comfort — so this is an important consideration.

A single skoolie occupant, or a skoolie family with a kid, may want to incorporate a twin mattress or a cot. A twin mattress is just 38 inches wide by 75 inches long, and a cot can be as narrow as 30 inches. Also, custom sizes of foam mattresses can be ordered online, or foam mattresses can be trimmed to whatever size you desire. I personally have dogs that like to sleep on the bed, so a queen mattress is a must for me. A king-size mattress is a whopping 6 feet 3 inches wide . . . perhaps a little much for a skoolie, but that's up to you!

Right: A bedroom at the back of the bus allows for storage space under the bed that can be accessed through the rear emergency door. **Above:** wooden panels slide back to reveal bunk beds.

41

Kitchen

How much kitchen space will you need? Ample kitchen space is a luxury for skoolies and can be hard to fit in. Think compact: a single sink saves counter space over a double sink, and overhead shelving can act as storage for food, cups, and plates. You'll also need to fit the refrigerator or cooler, stove, and microwave into the design. If you plan to do a lot of grilling outside your bus, you might want to locate your indoor kitchen close to the bus entrance.

Most recreational vehicles, campers, and tiny homes have kitchen counters no longer than 4 or 5 feet, not counting space for a small oven. A good tip is to utilize a standard bathroom vanity base in place of conventional kitchen base cabinets. Vanities are the same height as kitchen cabinets (so the countertop will be at the standard height) but are several inches shallower, from front to back. You can add a custom countertop to the vanity top and install a small bar sink for the kitchen sink. Some bathroom vanities have rounded sinks that extend slightly beyond the countertop for added space and style. Likewise, "farmhouse" or apron-style kitchen sinks protrude slightly beyond the surrounding counter and are more square.

For a kitchen table, you could repurpose two original bus seats by facing one seat from each side of the bus toward the other and installing a tabletop between them. (You need to use seats from both sides because the outer edge

Bus kitchens don't have to be tiny, and there are many ways to design the kitchen layout to flow with the dimensions of a bus.

Gravity-fed sinks are simple, functional, and perfect for skoolie owners working with a small budget.

Kitchen appliances can be salvaged from campers and RVs and fitted into your skoolie.

This kitchen table easily folds away with hinges to maximize floor space when not in use.

of the seats is supported by the side rail of the bus, leaving just one side supported by legs.) If you have smaller seats salvaged from the back of the bus, you could utilize those as booth seats and save on width. You could also build a custom booth to your liking and include storage space under each seat. Another option is to mount the table to the wall, supporting it with hinges and a removable support leg so the table can be folded away when not in use.

Composting toilets eliminate the need for additional plumbing.

Shower stalls can be custom made to fit in small spaces.

Bathroom

A bus bathroom can be as simple or elaborate as you want. If you'd like to have a shower and toilet in your bus, you can use a large metal trough as a tub or install a small shower base with plastic shower walls (sold at home stores) custom-cut to fit the space. Alternatively, you may choose to save space and simply construct an outdoor shower instead. For a toilet, you can invest in a fancy composting setup, such as the Nature's Head toilet; use a camping toilet; or fabricate a do-it-yourself toilet, which saves a lot on cost and is easy to maintain (see chapter 10).

Storage

Storage space is not to be taken lightly. You'll be surprised at how much stuff you have to put in your skoolie. Clothing, electronics, supplies, tools, food, and many other items will need to be stored and secured against the movement of the bus.

Storage space under the bed is excellent for clothing containers or drawers, shoes, extra water jugs, and more. One way to arrange underbed storage is to divide it into front and rear sections, with the front being accessible from inside the bus and the rear being accessible from the rear emergency exit door.

You can store items under sofas. You can even remove the sofa's feet and place the sofa frame above a framed-in storage box or a set of drawers similar to those found on a captain's bed.

Shelving is an excellent use of the space over windows and around the perimeter of the bus where you won't be walking. It's critical that you add a small ledge, at least 2 inches tall, along the front edge of the shelf to keep items from falling when the bus is moving. (Similarly, it is wise to use small hook-and-eye latches to keep drawers from opening while you're driving.)

Installing shelves above the windows creates a lot of storage without the complications of fitting cabinets along the ceiling's curve.

When you're on the move, you can keep loose items on the bed. And it's handy to have a small cubby in the front of the bus for quickly tossing in regularly used items such as water bottles, hats, electronics, and cameras. I like to use reclaimed wooden crates for storage because they have a cool vintage farm look, they're sturdy, and they can be moved around easily and secured in place with bungee cords or a small ledge screwed down around the perimeter of the box. Or you could simply secure the storage crate to the floor with wood screws, making sure the screws aren't long enough to contact the bus's metal floor.

A large drawer under the bed can simply rest on the floor and be pulled out when needed. A basic latch will hold it in place while you're on the road.

A small solid-fuel stove can keep you toasty in the winter while also drying out the interior of the bus.

Cold Considerations

Whether you're just traveling for a weekend in winter or you're a full-timer who lives in a chilly climate, cold, wet weather greatly limits what you can do outside the bus. A woodstove is an excellent way to stay warm and cozy in winter. If you choose to add a woodstove, you need to plan your interior layout to allow space for the stove as well as for storing firewood. The woodstove should be located as close to the center of the bus as possible from front to back, and spaced far enough off the wall to allow the chimney pipe to go through the ceiling. Be careful to position the stove so that the chimney pipe doesn't hit any of the roof supports, as these cannot be cut.

Also, be aware that if you opt for thicker insulation for your floor or walls, your layout will have a narrower interior space and less headroom due to the insulation.

Outdoor Spaces

Don't feel limited to fitting everything inside; consider options for outside the bus! An outdoor shower can greatly simplify your plumbing setup and save space (and minimize interior condensation). A fold-down table attached to the outside wall can be a huge asset when weather allows for outdoor dining. A rear storage platform is a popular addition because it can carry a generator and propane tank and serve as a place to sit, relax, or change shoes when returning from a hike.

Adding an awning to the side of your bus will increase the footprint of your home. Used camper awnings can be found for cheap at RV salvage yards or through classified ads. A basic "easy-up" shelter is very useful as well and can be stored under the bed, on a rear deck, or inside the bus.

Get INSPIRED

One of the best ways to find ideas and tips for designing your skoolie layout is to look at other skoolies! Getting the most out of small living spaces is all about creativity and customization. There are a lot of truly great folks with skoolies out there, and each skoolie has a personal style and layout that works for its owner.

In good weather, the outside of a skoolie can be just as much a part of your home-on-wheels as the inside is.

LEXIS NOELLE

ADVENTURING WITH LOLA

@ADVENTURINGWITHLOLA

Lexis lives full-time in a four-window 1989 Blue Bird short bus named Lola. With roughly 75 square feet of living space, Lexis still manages to work from home, making custom handmade items to sell online.

Even though her bus is the smallest size available, Lexis found space for a small two-person round table, a sofa bed, and a tiny kitchen counter with a portable cooktop and toaster oven/coffeemaker combination unit.

ADVENTURING WITH LOLA

For a bathroom, Lexis closed in a small space in the rear of her skoolie for a portable toilet — she swaps the toilet for a portable shower kit when needed. When the bus isn't connected to the power grid with an extension cord, a battery bank charged by the bus's alternator (while driving) provides electricity to a water pump that pulls water from a 15-gallon tank.

DEMOLITION

This chapter covers one of the most important and challenging parts of building your skoolie. It may sound like fun, but "demoing" such a sturdy vehicle is no easy task. Demolition starts with removing the seats, followed by the floor and the wall and ceiling panels (as desired). Then there are odds and ends to remove as well as wiring issues to address. Demo details vary from bus to bus, but we'll cover the basic process and offer a lot of helpful pointers.

DEMO TOOLS *and* SAFETY EQUIPMENT

BEFORE YOU BEGIN tearing things off your bus, let's not forget about the need for personal protection equipment, aka PPE. At the very least, you should purchase safety glasses, gloves, hearing protection, and dust masks. A respirator mask with replaceable or reusable filters is much better than a simple dust mask, if it's in your budget.

The two most useful tools you'll need for the demo process are a power drill and an angle grinder. You don't have to spend a lot for each tool, but keep in mind that you get what you pay for. You can also find used tools, but I would avoid this option, especially with battery-powered tools. If you can budget for a cordless drill, be sure to get at least two batteries. On the other hand, if there's electricity available where you'll be demoing your bus, a corded drill/driver and extension cord will be cheaper, and you'll never have to wait for batteries to charge. Don't forget to pick up some drill and driver bits — you'll use the drill both for drilling holes and for removing and driving screws.

A standard corded angle grinder usually is the best way to go. Cordless angle grinders exist, but they're expensive and the batteries don't last long between charges. But if you

don't have power at your work site, cordless is probably your only option. Some tool manufacturers offer full lines of cordless tools that all use the same batteries. This means you might be able to get a cordless drill and angle grinder that share batteries and a charger. Be sure to get plenty of cutting wheels for your grinder, at least ten to start.

As for hand tools, you should have a standard and a metric set of socket wrenches, a combination wrench set, screwdrivers, a pry bar, and a couple pairs of locking pliers.

Using the proper protective equipment — such as gloves, a dust mask, and a face shield — while working on your bus is just as important as having the right tools.

Attach a cutting wheel to your angle grinder, to quickly cut through bolts.

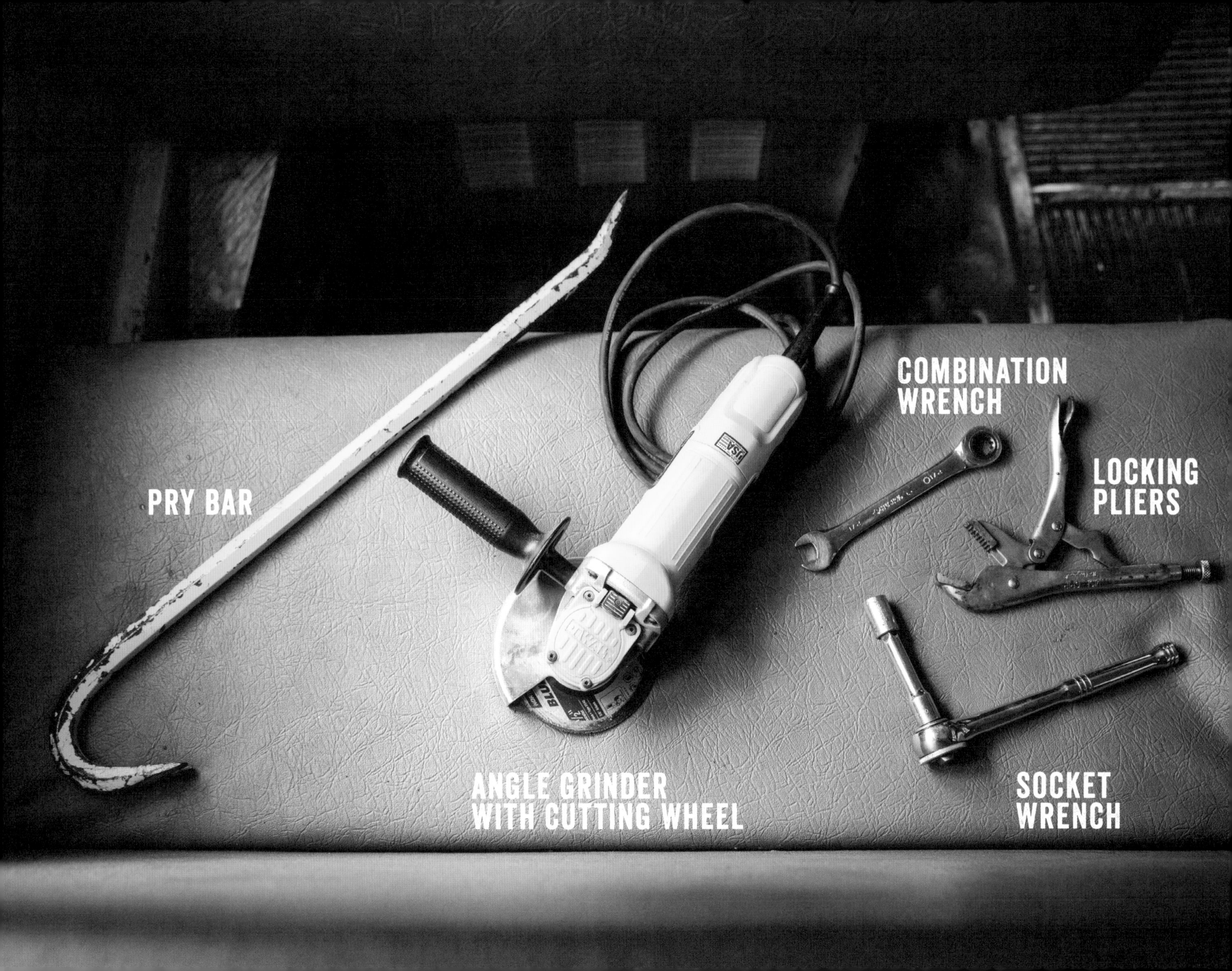

PRY BAR

COMBINATION WRENCH

LOCKING PLIERS

ANGLE GRINDER WITH CUTTING WHEEL

SOCKET WRENCH

REMOVING *the* SEATS

ONCE YOU HAVE proper PPE and tools, you're ready to start removing seats! In a perfect world, you would simply take a socket wrench and loosen the bolts from each seat, but, unfortunately, 99 percent of bus seats are a pain to remove. Think of it as a rite of passage for your skoolie conversion, and take your time removing them. If you have a midsize bus and take out two seats per day, you'll be done in a week!

It's possible to unbolt the seats, but each bolt has a nut underneath the bus that usually turns with the bolt as you try to loosen it, which means you're just wasting energy. You can climb under the bus, locate the nut and put locking pliers around it, then go back inside the bus and try to loosen the bolt. (Seats also may bolt to a rail along the side wall.) Sometimes this works, but many times the bolts are too corroded to turn, and they either

break off or the bolt head strips. This is where your angle grinder comes in handy!

With your PPE in place (particularly eye and ear protection), aim your angle grinder cutting wheel at the base of the bolts at a slight angle to slice into the bolt. Don't apply too much pressure, as this can damage the cutting wheel. Also, keep any combustible materials away from the sparks that will fly. The bolt will heat up as it's being cut, and once it's detached

Seats are bolted to the bus floor.

The quickest way to remove the bolts is to cut them off with an angle grinder.

Once the bolts have been cut away, the seat will come up easily.

Instead of using a cutting wheel, you can remove seat bolts with a socket wrench.

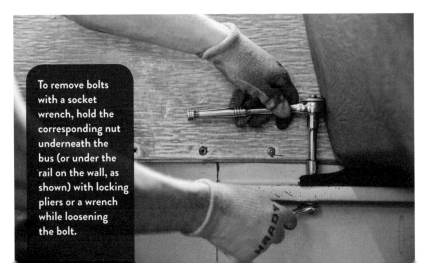

To remove bolts with a socket wrench, hold the corresponding nut underneath the bus (or under the rail on the wall, as shown) with locking pliers or a wrench while loosening the bolt.

Here's the full bolt with nut and washers.

Watch your canvas grow as each seat comes out. Getting all the seats out is a major feat and will give you a better idea of how much living space you'll have to work with.

the bolt head will be very hot, so don't pick it up right away! In addition, the rubber floor in buses can smoke some from the heat and release harmful vapors, so be sure to keep the bus well ventilated (this is one time where a respirator is especially useful). Keeping a small fan running beside you during seat removal helps a ton.

Another option for cutting out bus seats is to first cut the seats' legs, allowing you to remove the seat to make accessing the leg bolts easier. Don't do this if you plan to repurpose the seats.

A good tip for removing seats is to take a car jack, such as a standard bottle jack, place it under the seat frame, and jack up the seats to apply pressure on the bolts. Sometimes this can help keep the nuts from spinning when you are trying to loosen the bolts, but it's still likely that the nuts will spin along with the bolt. A bottle jack can also help break loose bolts when the grinder doesn't fully remove the bolt head or when a heated bolt melts and sticks to the hole on the seat frame.

When you get the first seat out of your bus, pat yourself on the back and enjoy the new-found open space. As each seat comes out, the reward for your hard work is seeing your canvas take shape.

If you are unable to remove the seats on your own, you can always find a mechanic or local handyperson willing to cut the seat bolts away for you.

Passenger HEATERS

WHEN YOU'RE REMOVING the seats, you may find a heater or two under one or more of the seats. These heaters use coolant/antifreeze from the engine to generate heat that radiates into the passenger area. Some heaters also have electric blowers and wiring. You can remove a heater so it's not interrupting your floor plan, or you can leave it in place and get free heat whenever the bus's engine is running. If you decide to keep the heater in the bus, the only downside is having to work it into your layout.

To remove a heater, you first have to disconnect the coolant input and output hoses and connect them together to bypass the heater. You make the connection with a barbed union fitting for hoses. Barbed unions are made of heavy-duty plastic and come in various sizes. Coolant hoses are typically ¾ inch to 1 inch, and the barbed union must fit your hose size.

Underneath the bus, below where the heater is located, you will see two black hoses going up through the bus floor and connecting to the bottom inputs of the heater with clamps (usually hose clamps). Use locking pliers to pinch the hoses closed, clamping the pliers a couple inches away from the ends so there's room to fit on the barbed union. Then, wearing rubber gloves to prevent engine coolant from coming into contact with your skin, loosen the hose

Remove the heaters after the seats have come out, to completely open up the interior.

Leftover power wires from the heater can be capped with wire nuts and tucked out of the way.

clamp on the input hose with a flat-head screwdriver and slip the clamp out of the way. Slowly and carefully pull the hose from the heater input. Insert one end of the barbed union all the way into the open end of the hose, and secure the hose over the union with the clamp. Repeat this step with the other hose from the heater to connect it to the other end of the union.

Some buses run the coolant lines along the bottom of the wall inside the bus rather than underneath. In this case, you can either leave the hoses in place after removing the heater and connecting the hose ends, or you can cut the hoses closer to the front of the bus and connect the hose ends there. Also, coolant lines that run inside usually have a small metal tunnel for protection. This can be removed with an angle grinder if it's riveted down, or with a screwdriver if it's screwed down.

WARNING: Be prepared for coolant spillage. It's a good idea to have a 5-gallon bucket handy to catch any coolant that spills from inside the heater. You can then pour it into a container (a recycled plastic jug will do) and take it to a hazard materials recycling center. *Do not* pour it down your sink or on the ground outside. Conventional coolant is highly toxic to animals, so keep it away from your pets.

Some buses have faucet-style valves under the hood that stop the flow of coolant to the passenger heaters, and others have valves near the driver's seat. If you can find any type of shutoff valve, close the valve before removing the heater(s) and leave it closed since it will no longer be used.

Once the heater is bypassed, you can unbolt it, or grind off the bolts, and remove the heater permanently. If the fan has wiring, cap off the wires with wire nuts (wire connectors) and secure them out of the way. Finally, check your coolant reservoir level (in the engine compartment) in case you need to replace coolant lost during the heater bypass procedure. If necessary, top it up with coolant/antifreeze that is labeled for universal use with other brands or coolant colors/types (not all coolants are interchangeable). Don't reuse the old coolant you captured in a bucket.

What to Do WITH BUS GUTS?

Metal seat frames with plywood, vinyl, and cushioning, along with the rubber flooring, wood subflooring, and metal walls and all the cut-away nuts and bolts, can really pile up. Some recycling centers will pay cash for scrap metal, but most recycling facilities won't take bus seats unless they're stripped down to the metal. Anything other than the metal guts of a bus will have to be disposed of. Large construction bags work well for the floor rubber, but you will have to cut it into smaller, more manageable sections. The wood subfloor from the bus will likely not be reusable because of old glue and moisture stains. You can cut it into smaller pieces to bag and have hauled away, or you can have the complete pieces hauled away.

Use a power drill or a grinder to remove the rivets or screws that attach the wall panels to the bus frame.

WALL *and* CEILING PANELS

REMOVING THE WALL panels in your bus can be as easy as unscrewing a ton of Phillips screws or as challenging as grinding or drilling out a ton of rivets. Regardless, it is in your best interest to remove the original thin metal interior siding to inspect for rust, allow for better insulation, and open up many options for custom wall paneling!

If you feel your bus walls are suitable as is, it's not a major no-no for a skoolie to keep its original wall panels, but you should still consider adding some form of additional thermal layering, such as radiant insulation. One option that many skoolie remodelers employ is to install framing over the original wall panels and add new insulation between the framing before covering it all with new paneling.

If you decide to demo the factory wall panels in your bus, the process is more repetitive than challenging. If you have screws, simply remove all of them one by one. If some are stubborn, you may have to cut them away with your grinder. If the siding is attached with rivets, you will have to cut them off, drill them out, or punch them out with a rivet pin punch and hammer. If you are fortunate enough to have access to an air compressor and an air-chisel tool, this is the ultimate way to remove rivets!

I personally prefer grinding rivets out, but if you do this, be sure to protect your windows from metal sparks, which can stick to the glass. The technique I use is to open the window and drape a damp towel over it so the towel covers the inside of the glass.

Some buses have wall paneling that folds under the window sill, in which case you can use the cutting wheel on your grinder to cut off the lower section of paneling. Make the cut 2 to 3 inches below the windows; this will allow you to insert new insulation under the windows.

Once you have the original wall paneling removed, you will most likely see some ugly old insulation behind it. Simply remove this by hand, wearing gloves, a mask or respirator, and eye protection. And keep the area well ventilated . . . old insulation is nasty!

Demolishing the original ceiling panels is done exactly the same way as the wall panels. I should mention that not every skoolie owner replaces the ceiling. Many people are happy with the metal ceiling in their buses and leave them as is. But a lot of air temperature is lost and gained through the ceiling, so you might want to replace the old insulation with newer, more efficient insulation. You could also use double-sided tape or glue to hold some thin radiant insulation against the original bus ceiling and then cover that with a finish material, such as wood running along the length of the bus. It all comes down to personal preference and budget.

In buses where the wall panel runs under/into the window itself, the panel can be trimmed off with a cutting wheel, just below the window.

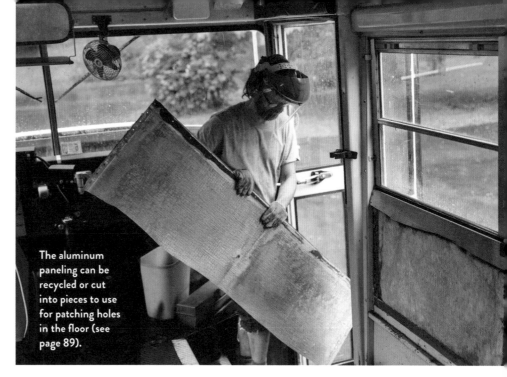

The aluminum paneling can be recycled or cut into pieces to use for patching holes in the floor (see page 89).

Be sure to wear gloves and a dust mask when you remove the old fiberglass insulation behind the wall panels.

The empty walls are ready to receive new foam insulation.

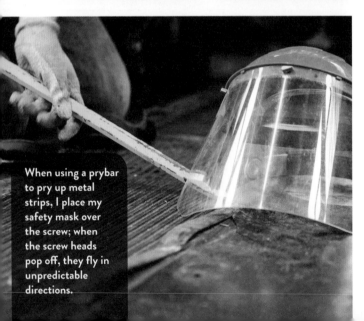

The metal strips along the aisle can be unscrewed with a drill, removed with a pry bar, or cut off with a grinder. Any remaining screws can be ground off.

When using a prybar to pry up metal strips, I place my safety mask over the screw; when the screw heads pop off, they fly in unpredictable directions.

FLOOR PREP

REMOVING THE FLOOR of your bus is important for two main reasons. First, you don't want to build your skoolie over a floor that may be rotted and rusty. Second, removing the original floor allows you to add a new insulated surface to help maintain a comfortable temperature inside. Insulation also cuts down on road noise when driving.

That said, if you are absolutely certain your bus floor is free of rust, corrosion, and rotted wood, and an entirely new floor doesn't fit your budget or time frame, you can leave the original floor intact. In this case, I would put down a roll of radiant insulation over the top of the original floor and underneath your new surface flooring. Radiant insulation acts as a light thermal jacket, maintaining some of the interior temperature and reflecting some exterior temperatures that would otherwise enter. Radiant insulation doesn't perform as well as rigid foam insulation to slow temperature transfer.

Most school buses have a top floor layer of thick rubber over ½-inch or ¾-inch plywood that sits on top of the primary metal floor. Some buses have only the rubber on top of the primary metal floor. The "walkway" down the center of the bus will be bordered with thin metal strips over the rubber. You can pry up the strips, unscrew them, or cut them off with your grinder. Sometimes you will find similar metal strips along the sides of the bus at the bottom of the wall. These can be removed in the same fashion as the walkway strips.

Removing the rubber floor can be a dirty job, especially if moisture has settled underneath the rubber or if it was glued down. Put on some gloves and start prying up the rubber. It might tear in places. As you get the rubber to pull up, you can grab it and peel it back by hand. It helps to have someone prying along the bottom edge of the rubber as you pull.

Once the rubber is up, it's time to remove the plywood layer, if there is one (in our bus, there was no plywood — just rubber over metal). The plywood is usually glued to the metal in various shapes and sizes. Sometimes the plywood is screwed or bolted down, but in most scenarios the seat bolts themselves secured the plywood better than the glue. The pry bar is your tool of choice for this step, and a second pry bar doesn't hurt. Once you pry up an edge of each plywood piece, you can begin pulling the wood up by hand (be sure to wear gloves). Don't be surprised if the wood is brittle or soggy — and isn't it nice knowing your dwelling won't be on top of it?

Now you can rest assured there are no more floor layers to remove! And now you can evaluate the condition of the primary metal floor and determine what needs to be done prior to building on top of it. I'll cover this process in chapter 6.

Most buses have plywood under the rubber floor, but some just have the rubber directly on the metal. A prybar (or two) can work the rubber and plywood loose.

EMERGENCY DOOR **24**

Other DEMO ITEMS

SEVERAL OF THE remaining demo items involve wiring. In many cases, you can remove an item that has wiring running to it and simply cap off each wire with a wire nut to terminate the wire. Sometimes, however, wiring configurations are interconnected with the bus's starting system, so make sure the bus starts up after *each* wiring change. If the bus fails to start, you'll know which wire(s) caused the problem. Never work with wiring while the bus is running.

Keep in mind that bus batteries exert a lot of cold-cranking amps during startup, then quickly recharge while the engine is running. To prevent unnecessary stress on the batteries, let the bus run for a few minutes at a medium rpm (somewhere between 1,200 and 1,800 rpm) before shutting it down. This allows the batteries to recharge so they're ready for the next start.

Exterior Demo

Outside your bus, you'll have a few items to take care of. Usually a decommissioned school bus has already had its STOP arm and front swing-out passenger bar removed and its red-and-amber school bus alert lights painted over. If these tasks have not been done, take care of them now — for legal purposes.

Removing the STOP arm is pretty straightforward. The mechanism is held on with screws, and there will be wires running underneath it when you pull it off. You can cut those wires and use wire nuts to terminate the ends, then tuck the protected ends inside the hole they came out of. You can seal the hole with a dab of caulk.

You can remove the front swing-out bar and deal with the wiring just as with the STOP arm. Be sure to properly terminate the wires and keep them out of the way; you can reroute them under the hood where they can be secured and tucked aside.

Door Alarms

Emergency exit alarms, chimes, and buzzers are quite annoying, but they ensure your exits are all closed and alert you if something opens while the bus is running. Most skoolie owners remove these alarms by disconnecting the wiring. If you do this, make a note of which wires you're disconnecting so you can easily reconnect them in case the bus has a starting issue or develops a slow drain on the battery system, which would result in the engine turning over sluggishly due to weakened batteries.

In most cases, you can simply disconnect or cut the two wires and put a wire nut on the ends to terminate them. The alarm is normally triggered when the wires connect, so capping them off with wire nuts prevents the alarm from activating. Occasionally you will have an "interlock" setup with three wires, and you can disconnect the ground wire alone for each alarm to bypass the interlock setup.

Speakers and Lights

Overhead speakers were originally used for intercom systems, but they can be connected to a stereo. You may opt to leave these speakers in place, replace them with higher-quality units, or simply cover them up. Another option is to replace them with lights, which requires replacing the cabling (12- or 14-gauge wiring is sufficient for most 12-volt lighting; see Power Basics on page 146). If you are replacing the ceiling, you can easily install the new wiring after the original ceiling has been demoed. If you're not replacing the ceiling, adding wiring over the factory ceiling is challenging or impossible; in this case, lights along the sides of the bus where wiring can be located and concealed are best.

If your bus came with interior passenger lights, these may be grounded by the metal ceiling itself rather than a separate ground wire. In this case, a single power wire runs to each light, and each light housing is grounded to the metal ceiling. If you relocated these lights over wood, they would lose their grounding. To solve this issue, you could use a longer screw that goes through the wood and into the original metal mounting location, or you could attach a small wire between the metal roof framing and the light housing, using small machine screws and nuts for the housing and a small self-tapping screw (see Self-Tapping Screws on page 112) into the metal roof framing.

Window or Wall Channels

The windows on your bus will have a thin piece of metal between them that can be removed in the same fashion as the wall paneling, but sometimes the wall framing itself is the only thing visible. When you remove these sections of metal, you'll see a main support beam, which is typically a C- or U-style beam with the open side of the beam facing inward, toward the passenger area. This space will allow for insulation in the future, and it also provides access to screws that hold the windows in place.

Nearly all buses have a channel on each side, running over the windows, that houses some wiring for interior lights, the rear taillights, and other marker or signal lights. You can remove this only if you're willing and able to fashion a similar method of protecting this wiring. You can add wiring to this channel if you'd like, such as wiring for a backup camera or other 12-volt accessories.

Plastic or metal access panels are usually screwed into the back of the bus to allow for easier access to the taillights. If you decide to replace these panels with wood or any other material, it's best to maintain the ability to access the areas behind the panels.

Window CHANNELS

The upper walls above the window on a school bus are actually the roof itself, curving down to create a channel over the windows. Attached to this section of wall are the metal channels that conceal wires for the rear lights, door and hatch alarms, and interior lights. You can remove these channels to expose the wiring (usually there are screws or rivets holding the channels in place), or you can work around them. If you decide to remove them, be sure to leave space to prevent the existing wiring from getting pinched behind the new ceiling. Alternatively, you can use the channels to add new wiring for any 12-volt devices such as a backup camera, speakers, and the like.

In this bus, the framing between the windows is exposed, rather than being covered with thin metal. The horizontal clips across the frame member hold the windows in place.

MATT SLOANE
CAMP DAVID
@CAMPDAVID.OTR

Even though Matt's bus is just six windows long, it's built on a large International bus frame. Outside, Matt used a dark olive-green paint reminiscent of military vehicles. Attached to the exterior is an RV awning that adds additional usable space when the bus is parked. On the roof he installed a deck for storage and observation. The deck is all metal, including the metal mesh floor!

MATT SLOANE

CAMP DAVID

While the inside is just around 120 square feet, the bus still has a separate space for a composting toilet. The adorable kitchen space, anchored by a single kitchen cabinet base with a wooden counter, includes a small bar sink, a two-burner cooktop, and a small microwave oven mounted in an overhead bin. A single rear-facing bench seat is tucked against a table with a mini-fridge placed underneath. A queen-size bed is across the back of the bus, with additional storage cabinets overhead (there's even a closet). Keep an eye out for the Camp David bus!

⑤ *exterior* MAKEOVER

The most recognizable feature of a school bus is its deep yellow paint job. Although this color is one of my favorites, it's totally understandable if you wish to repaint your skoolie. Some states require you to change the paint scheme on retired school buses, in addition to painting over the "school bus" lettering on the front and back. If you choose not to repaint, you can doll up your bus by removing old stickers and touching up the old paint as needed. You can paint the bus at any time — before, during, or after the conversion. You can even repaint it if you have a change of heart; after all, it's your bus!

Options for PAINTING A SCHOOL BUS

THERE ARE CHEAP and expensive options for painting a bus. Painting with brushes and rollers is a thrifty approach; spraying will yield smoother, shinier results. Another option, of course, is a professional paint job. If your bus is properly prepped for paint, though, you can achieve a respectable DIY paint job for a fraction of the cost of what a professional would charge.

Alternatives to brushing and rolling include air-powered spray guns (also known as air sprayers), HVLP (high volume, low pressure) electric airless sprayers, and standard spray-paint "rattle cans." If you opt for an air-powered gun, you can rent a small "pancake" air compressor and buy a cheap air sprayer paint gun from a discount tool retailer, like Harbor Freight. The advantage of HVLP electric sprayers is that they don't require an air compressor and they typically hold up longer than cheaper air sprayers. I've had good luck with cheap air sprayers for one use, but I don't expect them to work as well for future uses.

Some paints are available both in standard form and in aerosol spray cans. This means you can paint your bus with the regular paint and buy a few cans of the spray paint for touch-ups later. I also like to keep a can of black spray paint to touch up wheels and bumpers.

Choosing Paints and Colors

The next step is selecting paint! I'm sure you already have a color in mind, but let's take a moment to consider the roof paint first. The roof of your bus will see the most sun, so it makes sense to paint it with a reflective color, preferably white. Roofs also take a beating from rain, snow, hail, and so on and need the most protection. Special paints have been designed for recreational vehicles and buses; Bus-Kote and Anvil Roof-Tec are noteworthy brands. These are elastomeric paints (they create a rubberlike coating) and have reflective and insulating properties that reduce heat transfer to the inside of the bus. For this reason, they're sometimes called thermal paints. Because school bus yellow is such a strong color, it could take up to four coats of another color to cover the yellow, but if you put down an oil-based white coat first, you'll need fewer coats to finish the roof. Also, elastomeric paint can peel if scratched, which will expose the yellow roof underneath; again, a base coat of oil-based white paint disguises this. While thermal paint is ideal for your bus roof, if you don't use it, I strongly suggest you at least select an oil-based white paint designed for metal.

Choosing the primary body color for your bus is no different from picking out a color for your house, but you will definitely want an exterior-grade formula that works on metal. I prefer oil-based heavy-duty equipment paint (also sold as oil-based industrial enamel paint). This is designed for farm vehicles and other heavy equipment and is highly durable. Also, heavy-duty paints are available in spray-can versions ideal for occasional touch-ups. You will want to purchase enough paint to apply at least two coats if you're using brushes and rollers, but more coats will be needed if you use a paint sprayer. Paint sprayers usually achieve a nicer finish when the paint is applied in several thin layers. After your bus is painted, you can go back over the oil-based paint with a clear-coat finish that adds a protective layer and helps maintain the shine.

THERE ARE SO MANY OPTIONS FOR COLORS
AND WAYS TO PAINT YOUR BUS!

PREPPING *and* PAINTING YOUR BUS

AS WITH ANY paint job, quality results hinge on thorough prep work. Paint doesn't stick well to dirty, rough, rusty, or even glossy surfaces. Therefore, your prep should focus on cleaning and sanding the old paint and dealing with rust and rough patches so the new paint will bond properly and won't show old blemishes.

Cleaning It Up

Start your prep work by thoroughly removing old, unwanted stickers and decals. This can be more time consuming than you'd assume. Use a hair drier to heat the adhesive on old decals, then peel them away. And because glue fumes may be released by the heat, you should protect yourself with a respirator or at least a mask and good ventilation. Brake fluid or brake cleaner acts as a great solvent for the sticky residue left by old decals. Another option for more stubborn decals is an adhesive decal remover wheel that can attach to a power drill.

Once you have removed the old decals, rent a power washer or drive to a manual car wash (make sure the bus will fit in the bay before you drive in!) to get all the grime off the original paint. If a power washer is unavailable, you can scrub your bus with heavy-duty sponges and spray it with a garden hose and a high-pressure nozzle.

The next step is to remove any loose or flaking paint with a wire brush or a paint scraper. If you have surface rust spots, use those same tools to remove the loose rust before sanding and painting. Rust on metal has a tendency to come back, so keep track of any spots you have to clean up and address them all. You can also apply the same rust treatment materials and techniques that you use for the interior floor (see chapter 6) on exterior spots. Make sure the rust treatment is completely dry before painting the area. And if in removing rust you expose bare metal, use a metal primer to establish a base paint that the primary body paint will stick to.

Sanding, Sanding, Sanding

Sanding the original paint is crucial to a successful, lasting paint job. When you sand over the original paint, you create a better surface for the new paint to adhere to. Sandpapers are categorized by their grit number: the lower the number, the coarser or more aggressive the grit; the higher the number, the finer the grit. Sand your bus with 400-grit paper or up to a 600 grit. It's best to use sandpaper that's designed for wet sanding, which is less likely to leave scratches that show though the new paint. Wet sandpaper also stays cleaner during sanding. Fill a bucket or tray with water and mix in a little dish soap. Dip the sandpaper in the water periodically as you sand. This also helps clean the surface while you roughen the old finish.

For an alternative to sandpaper, use abrasive pads (such as Scotch-Brite), which will be gentler on the surface. These can be dampened with water as well.

When you are ready to sand, start at one end of the bus and work your way to the other end. Sand with consistent back-and-forth motions rather than circular movements: an even, back-and-forth pattern allows the paint to stick more consistently. Be sure to rewet the sandpaper or abrasive pad regularly. After you've finished

SANDING *Safety*

You will need at least a 6-foot ladder to reach the higher sections of the bus. Always exercise caution when working on the roof! When sanding, wear gloves and a mask or respirator because paint particles contain chemicals that are harmful if inhaled.

The first step in painting your bus is to thoroughly clean it. A pressure washer helps speed up the process and get the bus as clean as possible.

A hair dryer will help remove old stickers and decals. Wear a mask — the glue in the decals with release volatile compounds when heated!

Tape off lights and around windows to prevent any paint from accidentally getting on them.

sanding, the original bus paint should have a slightly dulled finish. Now rinse the bus thoroughly with plain water, working from top to bottom, to remove all sanding dust.

Taping Off

There's one more prep step: properly taping off the areas you don't want to paint, such as windows, trim, wheels, and the like. Use ordinary blue painter's tape and old newspapers or plastic sheeting to protect these areas. It helps to have a friend on the other end of the tape or plastic to keep it straight when applying.

If you don't want to get paint on the ground surface below and around the bus, cover it with tarps. Sprayed paint goes *everywhere* and can fly pretty far — even without a breeze. For this reason, don't paint your bus near a house, fence, or other structure you don't want to get paint on.

Paint Application

Applying the paint can be done with an electric airless sprayer, an air sprayer, or standard paint rollers and brushes. Paint sprayers may seem expensive, but quality paint brushes and rollers aren't that cheap, either! Paint is usually poured into a reservoir tank attached to the sprayer, although some sprayers have a small hose that feeds paint directly from the paint can to the sprayer. Electric sprayers plug into a regular household outlet via an extension cord; air sprayers use compressed air to discharge the paint rather than electricity (but the compressor runs on electricity).

Paint sprayers are time consuming to clean after you've finished painting, and, unfortunately, they don't always perform properly in the future if they aren't cleaned extremely well. For this reason, some people prefer to purchase a cheap electric sprayer and use it only once.

Remember: Spray painting requires full masking and taping off of any areas you don't want painted. Overspray from paint sprayers is hard to avoid, so take your time when masking.

Alternatively, painting with rollers and brushes is a perfectly fine way to paint your bus. Because buses have mostly flat surfaces, rolling the paint is much like painting a wall, only the surface is metal rather than drywall. While rollers can get the large spaces, the many nooks and crannies will have to be painted with a brush.

Traditional rollers and brushes can be used to put on a fresh coat of paint.

A quality brush will make painting your bus easier and will be less likely to lose brush hairs in the paint.

PAINT APPLICATION TIPS

- Gather a variety of brushes and rollers, from small to large, and don't skimp on brush quality.

- Use sturdy paint trays; you don't want a flimsy tray when working on a ladder.

- Keep a can of brush cleaner or mineral spirits handy as well as a few old rags for cleaning up unwanted paint drips.

- You can call friends to help. A third or fourth set of hands can save you a ton of time.

- Check the forecast. Don't start painting your bus on a day when it's likely to rain. Even better: have an escape plan to get your bus under shelter if necessary.

- Don't remove the painter's tape before the paint has had a chance to dry; otherwise, the paint can peel off.

- Read and follow the directions on the paint can. Not all paints are created equal. Temperature, humidity, and other application conditions (such as painting in shade vs. sun) can affect how the paint is applied.

- Wear rubber gloves and long sleeves if you don't want paint getting on your bare skin. It can take weeks for paint to wear off.

- When spraying paint, always wear a mask and eye protection. The paint can potentially blow back at you if a sudden gust of wind comes along. Wearing old clothes or disposable coveralls might be smart protection from paint drift and overspray, too.

OTHER WAYS TO TRICK OUT YOUR SKOOLIE

Another option, which we used for our Woody Bus, is simply to add boards to the sides. On this bus, the paint was in good shape, so we decided to add flair by making it look like a vintage Woody station wagon. We liked it so much, we did the same thing for our Willbillys bus.

DEAN CHYTRAUS
THE SKOOLIE
@THESKOOLIE

Dean lives full time in his 1994 GMC eight-window, midsize bus. Dean has traveled all over the United States and Canada, making a home on public lands, in RV parks, in state and national parks, in neighborhoods, in parking lots, at truck stops, by the ocean, in deserts, in forests, and more!

Outside, the bus features a desert-tan paint job with custom-painted trees on the sides and large decks at the rear and on the roof. For power, four 100-watt solar panels on the roof charge four deep-cycle batteries.

Inside there is a small kitchen with a table booth, a large sink, a 12-volt cooler, and a stainless steel two-burner cooktop. The bus features a Nature's Head composting toilet and a 30 × 30-inch shower stall. A 9,000-Btu mini-split system installed in the rear of the bus keeps the skoolie cool on hot days.

6

PREPPING *for* CONSTRUCTION

With your bus gutted and the interior surface materials out of the way, you now have a much clearer view of any rust and corrosion issues, and you're ready to prepare your "blank canvas" for its new finishes. You'll start with the floor, which usually needs the most work, then you'll seal up the walls and windows and finish with a quick check of the ceiling.

It's very common to find rust around the entrance area of a bus, where there's a lot of foot traffic.

CLEANING *and* PAINTING THE FLOOR

EVALUATING THE METAL floor of your bus is the next step. Hopefully, you have little to no floor rust to deal with, but we all know the likelihood of this is low. Surface rust will be easy to handle in most cases: bus floors are thick, and there is enough metal there that you can grind off superficial rust spots and still have a very solid surface.

Typically, rust spots are found at the front and back of the bus around the wheel wells, and around the individual holes that the seat bolts passed through.

GRIND OFF THE SURFACE RUST. To tackle rusty areas, use a wire brush or a wire-brush attachment for your grinder or drill and go over the top of the rust spots until you reach a solid, nonrusted metal surface. Be sure to wear a respirator or mask and eye and ear protection as well as long sleeves, and use a fan to blow the dusty air out of the bus. Go over the entire bus floor with the same wire brush to remove dirt, grime, and leftover glue residue.

ADDRESS MORE SERIOUS RUST ISSUES. Don't expect the floor to appear shiny and new once you've wire-brushed it, but you should see the brown and coarse rusty surface begin to smooth over. If you find areas with large flakes of rust and the floor feels soft or flexes as you put weight on it, you likely have a much more serious rust issue. Test to see how solid the rust spot is by poking it with a screwdriver. If the screwdriver goes through the floor, you will need to cut away the rusted metal with a grinder, then patch the hole with new metal. If the hole is smaller than 5 inches, you can patch over it with thin scrap metal and metal adhesive, such as JB Weld. Make sure the patch is a few inches larger than the hole, so there's plenty of margin for adhesive. Holes 5 inches or larger should be covered with a welded patch that is flush with the floor rather than resting or overlapping on top of the surrounding metal. In any case, let's hope your original inspection of the bus was accurate and there are no serious rust issues!

A wire brush attached to an angle grinder will help remove surface rust.

Thoroughly vacuum up dust and debris after grinding.

Spray rusty spots on the floor with a rust converter.

Once all rust has been treated, the floor is ready for paint.

POR-15 is a popular rust treatment coating that can be applied over areas that show signs of rust.

TREAT WITH RUST CONVERTER. After you have wire-brushed the entire floor, taken care of rust spots, and vacuumed up the debris, you must treat those rusted areas with a rust converter, a product designed to restore metal surfaces to prevent future rust. Rust is like cancer: the sooner you stop it, the better! The most common rust restoration product is POR-15. Others include "1" Step Rust Killer, Ospho metal treatment, and Loctite Naval Jelly. All of these products work in a similar way but have specific application instructions. POR-15's multistep process requires several different products sold individually or in complete kits. I have found that a 1-pint kit from POR-15 works well for a midsize bus with an average amount of surface rust. (By "average" I mean surface rust around each bolt hole in the floor and around the rear wheel humps.) Treating each rust spot, plus the area around the spot, will be fine; there's no need to apply rust converter over areas that have no rust issues.

PATCH THE HOLES. The next step is to fill in or patch over the holes where the seat bolts were. You can use 100-percent silicone caulk to fill in the holes; cut small pieces of thin metal and silicone them in place over the holes (metal from the interior walls you removed works, too); or use pennies and silicone (leave them heads-up for good luck!). Some floor holes can be as large as ½ inch, others as small as ⅛ inch. The larger holes are better covered with metal pieces or pennies, and the smaller holes are okay to fill with silicone. You *must* cover these holes because they go through to the underside of the bus, and you don't want moisture, road salt, cold air, and other debris coming in contact with your new floor.

PAINT THE FLOOR. When all holes are covered and the silicone has completely cured (curing usually takes 24 hours), your floor is now ready for a coat of paint. If you have left-over exterior paint, this will work for your floor as well. There's no need to worry about its color because it will eventually be covered. One coat will work to cover the floor, as the floor will never be exposed to the sun or weather. Rust-Oleum is one brand of oil-based paint for the metal floor. Other oil-based paints will work as well, such as Majic or Sherwin-Williams Industrial Enamel.

Why Not LEARN TO WELD?

Most auto mechanics have access to a welder or know of someone who can weld, so that's a great starting point for finding someone to lend a hand with your repairs. Or consider taking a welding class — it's an excellent way to learn a skill that most people lack, and a nice MIG-style welder, a welding gas tank, and welding accessories are reasonably priced. You can also watch training videos online. Personally, learning to weld was one of the best decisions in my life!

After treating rust spots, leftover seat bolt holes can be covered with pieces of metal glued down over the hole. Coins work, too! Larger openings can be covered with leftover sections of metal from the wall panels.

SEALING WALLS, WINDOWS, *and* CEILING

After testing to see how watertight the windows are, remove failed caulking and re-caulk around the window exterior.

ONCE YOUR FLOOR is dry, inspecting the walls is the next step. You're less likely to have rust issues in your walls than in your floors, but it's important to check before building over them. Inspect the wall framing for rust and corrosion. If you find any spots, treat them in the same fashion as the rust spots on the floor, wire-brushing to remove the rust, then treating with a rust converter. If rust is present, it usually occurs around the bottoms of the walls and around the wall side supports. The side supports are sometimes referred to as the ribs because they continue from the sides of the bus, between the windows (where they are considered window pillars), and up over the bus, also functioning as roof supports, almost like a rib cage for the vehicle. In most cases, the windows will be the source of moisture getting in the walls and causing rust.

School bus windows aren't exactly energy efficient and are arguably terrible for maintaining comfortable temperatures inside the bus, but most skoolies get by just fine using them.

(You also have the option of tinting or covering windows, or removing them and replacing them with metal. See Tinting or Covering Bus Windows on page 107.) Inspect your bus's windows thoroughly for leaks, which happen when the exterior caulk around them ages and dries out or peels away, allowing rainwater to seep in. If you see failed caulking, remove all the remaining old caulk and add fresh caulk rather than trying to patch the existing caulk. (Caulk sticks to almost anything, but it doesn't stick well to itself.) Once the caulk is completely dry, test the windows with a hose to make sure the caulk creates a complete seal. The most important place to caulk is along the bottom of the exterior windowsills, where the window frame meets the bus body. That said, caulking around

the entire exterior window is a great preventive measure.

You will also use caulk to seal around any leaky roof emergency exits. Caulking can be found in many different brands at any hardware store or home center. I've had great luck with DAP clear silicone caulk, which is capable of sticking to wet surfaces, so if it rains right after you've caulked, no worries!

If you've gone over your windows and confirmed that they aren't leaking, but you still see trickles of water coming down the walls, there are several possible causes. One is an exterior rivet that has broken or worked loose, such as a rivet securing one of the rub rails in place. You can apply caulking over the top of this spot or remove and replace the loose rivet. Water also can work its way between pieces of metal that join together on the exterior. On some buses, the pillars that go between the windows run behind the exterior metal panels, below the window at the point where they meet along the bottom of the windows, which means water could get in. You can put caulking over this joint, but be sure to test it once the caulking is dry.

Checking for Ceiling Leaks

Bus ceilings require minimal preparation for construction compared to floors and walls. You're not likely to find rust spots on your ceiling (if you chose to remove the interior panels), but it's possible to have leaks around roof emergency exits. You can test the roof emergency exits with a hose or simply watch for seepage during a rainy day. These leaks can be caused by worn rubber gaskets around the exit hatch or from old caulking around the exit fixture. Remove and replace the old caulking or replace the rubber hatch gaskets to solve this common leaking problem.

If resealing the hatch doesn't stop the leak, you may have to remove the exit altogether and cover the opening with a piece of sheet metal riveted or screwed down — with silicone caulk applied between the original roof and the new metal to create a watertight seal. Alternatively, you can replace the exit hatch with an exhaust fan (see page 172) permanently mounted on the roof.

Over time, caulking will dry and crack away, causing leaks — especially around roof hatches. It's best to remove the old stuff and apply fresh caulk.

OUR "US BUS"
THE WOODY BUS

Sabrina and I built the Woody Bus on a tight budget in two months' time, not long after we met. We both decided a short bus would be perfect for us, and the owner of a local bar agreed to sell us his "drunk bus," which was no longer being used, for a very reasonable price.

To save money, we built a gravity-fed sink, carpeted the floor, and used reclaimed kitchen cabinets from our neighbor. We had the bus finished by December, and by February, we were on the road (despite a snowstorm that left 40 inches of snow the week before we left!). We were in Oregon within four days and stopped to visit relatives and friends along the way — so fun!

OUR "US BUS"
THE WOODY BUS

We met our first skoolie friends in the redwoods in California. We quickly adapted to living in the 76-square-foot space, and after covering almost 8,000 miles, we realized that the skoolie lifestyle was definitely for us!

After our big trip, we continued using the Woody Bus for local trips and long-term guests. We soon found a newer bus that was seven feet longer, though, and we had to have it. We sold the Woody Bus to a friend of ours who has taken the bus cross-country twice.

7

INSULATION and FLOORING

While you likely discovered some insulation when removing your wall and ceiling panels, it's safe to say this was neither a noteworthy amount nor a quality material. In most cases, you'll get much better energy performance — and therefore will be more comfortable — if you replace the old insulation with new material before buttoning up the walls, ceiling, and floor. At the end of the insulation phase, you'll also install subflooring so that you're ready for additional wall framing or built-ins (chapter 8) or for the final floor, wall, and ceiling finishes.

What Kind of
INSULATION IS BEST?

THE THICKNESS OF the insulation you can install will depend on the depth of the wall cavity. Most buses have wall cavities roughly 2 inches deep; however, that distance can vary slightly even in the same bus, so it's safer to install a slightly thinner insulation type, such as 1½-inch-thick foam-board insulation panels. If you plan to add framing studs to the walls of your bus for the new wall paneling to attach to (rather than attach the paneling directly to the side wall supports, just like the original metal walls), you will be creating a deeper wall cavity, which will allow for thicker insulation.

Once the studs are installed, measure the total depth of the wall cavity to determine the maximum thickness of insulation for that location. Also, if you are adding wall framing studs, you should drill holes in the studs for any electrical wiring and water lines to pass through *before* you install the wall paneling or other finish material.

Insulation Types

Traditional batt or blanket insulation performs like a puffy down coat. It relies on trapped air to slow temperature transfer from one side of the insulation to the other. The thicker and fluffier the insulation, the more air is trapped, and the better the insulation performs. Likewise, the thinner or more compressed the insulation is, the worse it tends to perform. In fact, compressed insulation, no matter how thick it starts out, loses a considerable amount of its insulating ability, or R-value.

Because there are only a couple inches of space between the inner and outer walls of a bus, traditional insulation is too thin (and may be too compressed) to do much good in this application. Due to the compression issue, it would be senseless to forcefully stuff a bunch of thick R-30 insulation into the small space between the walls of your bus.

Long story short: traditional batt or blanket insulation is *not* the best choice for your skoolie. Fortunately, a few other types work quite well. The standard and best all-around option is rigid foam insulation board. Alternatively, you can use spray foam insulation (though it's pricey). And if you don't have room for true insulation, you can at least install a radiant insulation barrier to help keep out heat.

RIGID INSULATION BOARDS come in various thicknesses. The R-value of the board increases with thickness and ranges from about R-4 to R-8 per inch. For example, a 2-inch-thick board at R-5 per inch has a total R-value of R-10.

Thicker insulation is obviously preferred if you have the wall clearance, but not everyone has the luxury of added ceiling insulation thickness due to clearance restraints. It's important to keep in mind the thickness of the floor insulation, subfloor, final floor, and both ceiling insulation and paneling to avoid ending up with a ceiling that is so low that you can't stand fully upright.

Almost all rigid insulation board is load-bearing and designed to function under concrete floors, foundations, and even roadways. This means you can install your wood subfloor right on top of it.

There are three common types of rigid insulation: extruded polystyrene (XPS), expanded polystyrene (EPS), and polyisocyanurate (poly-iso or ISO).

I have found XPS and EPS insulation to be the easiest to cut, and both come in load-bearing varieties measured in pounds per square inch (psi). You can buy polyiso insulation with load-bearing capabilities, but it tends to crumble along the edges when it's cut. Overall, I prefer XPS because it's easy to handle.

SPRAY-FOAM INSULATION is one alternative to rigid insulation panels. Spray-foam kits are available in different "board foot" sizes

Rigid insulation panels can be scored with a utility knife and snapped off, creating the right size needed to fit into the wall framing.

Expanding foam in a spray can is great for filling in leftover spaces around the insulation panels. After it dries, any excess foam is easy to cut away. It's also very sticky, so be sure to wear gloves.

at a relatively high cost, but they do a great job of thoroughly covering walls and ceilings. Spray foam kits come with pressurized nitrogen that blows the insulation foam onto the surface that you want insulated, such as your bus walls.

Spray foam insulation has the potential to reach hard-to-get corners and crevices in the walls and ceiling, whereas foam-board insulation is difficult to fit perfectly into odd spaces. Spray foam kits typically come with everything you need, including gloves and a plastic outfit to prevent the insulation from getting on you.

To prepare the bus for insulating with spray foam, you must cover any areas of the interior (such as windows) that are typically vulnerable to overspray.

Once the insulation is applied and has dried, you trim excess insulation from the wall or ceiling so the insulation is flush with the framing or supports to allow the finish material to lie flat (in houses, spray foam that bubbles out of wall cavities is trimmed back so it is flush with the studs).

I don't suggest using spray insulation for the floor, but if you decide to go this route, you will need to frame in the floor with boards that the subfloor will attach to. Spray insulation is commonly used for ceilings because the foam readily conforms to ceiling curves. By comparison, rigid insulation board requires much more cutting and gap-filling to make the curve.

RADIANT INSULATION is akin to wearing a jacket rather than a coat. If you need to preserve as much ceiling clearance as possible, or if you plan to be nomadic and follow good weather, radiant "reflective" insulation might be your best option.

Radiant insulation is sold in large rolls and can be installed with glue or double-sided tape. Seams between rows of insulation should be taped to create an air seal. Radiant insulation comes in three styles: a single sheet of reflective plastic, two sheets of reflective plastic with a single layer of air bubbles between, or two sheets of reflective plastic with a double layer of air bubbles between. The air bubbles slow the transfer of heat, making the insulation more effective. Typical radiant insulation reflects around 94 percent of radiant energy created by the sun or other heat sources. In winter, radiant insulation will help contain the heat from your woodstove within your skoolie.

Radiant insulation is like a light jacket — it's best for skoolies in mild climates or those that won't be used as a primary dwelling.

DO I NEED A *Vapor Barrier?*

A vapor barrier is a water-impermeable membrane (such as thick plastic) that is used in some home construction to keep water vapor from migrating into wall and floor cavities, where it can become trapped and condense, leading to mold, rot, and other problems. Depending on the climate, a home may have vapor barriers keeping indoor moisture from going out or keeping outdoor moisture from coming in.

In a bus, the metal floor and sides of the bus act as a vapor barrier, so there's no need for additional barriers. In fact, adding a vapor barrier can cause moisture to become trapped among the wall or floor layers, potentially causing a host of moisture problems.

Installing RIGID INSULATION

THE BASIC PROCESS of installing rigid insulation is to measure each space where it is going to be placed and use a ruler and marker to draw cutting lines on the insulation board. Then, use a utility knife to score along the cutting lines (you can use the ruler as a straightedge to help make a straight score). Finally, snap the insulation along the scored lines to break off the waste. Snapping it off is quite satisfying, like a karate chop!

TO INSULATE YOUR BUS FLOOR:
Measure the full width of the floor from side to side. If the floor is 90 inches wide and your rigid insulation is 96 inches long, you simply have to score and snap the insulation boards to fit; you'll run the insulation boards across the bus, perpendicular to the bus sides. Any left-over pieces come in handy when you're insulating the walls, thus maximizing the usage you get from the insulation boards.

You'll have to make custom cuts to fit the insulation between the wheel humps (turn to page 117 to see how to insulate over the wheel humps). You can apply construction adhesive to the bottom of the insulation boards to keep them in place while you're working on top of them prior to the subfloor installation. If you have anything heavy, such as sandbags, place these on top of the insulation boards to hold them down while the glue dries.

Once you have the floor covered with the insulation, use seal tape to cover the cracks between the individual boards. Now the floor is ready for subflooring!

TO INSULATE YOUR WALLS: Cut each piece of rigid insulation to size and fit it into place inside the wall cavities, then use canned expanding spray foam (such as Great Stuff) to fill in the gaps around the insulation and to keep it in place.

Expanding spray foam is easy to use but may be the stickiest, messiest stuff in the world. It comes in aerosol cans and is designed to weatherize a home by sealing cracks. Different formulas offer different levels of foam expansion. For this application, use a low-expanding foam. Wait a couple hours to allow it to dry fully before touching it, at which point you can cut off the excess expanded foam. I prefer to use a dinner knife as a miniature saw to make a nice clean edge when cutting the foam away.

TO INSULATE YOUR CEILING:

Assuming you've removed the original ceiling, the process of installing new insulation boards is slightly different from the wall application. Because the ceiling curves, the insulation boards must be cut into narrow pieces and placed side by side on the ceiling, allowing them to follow the curve. If the ceiling's framing is a solid square, with no channel to slide the edges of the insulation boards into to hold them in place, you can instead make the sections of insulation about ¼ inch oversize and wedge them between the framing. You can also use construction adhesive to help hold them in place. Cover small gaps between the boards with seal tape, and use expanding spray foam for larger gaps. Just be on the lookout for spray foam drips falling from the ceiling; you don't want that stuff in your hair!

After trimming insulation panels to fit across the floor, you can glue them down with heavy-duty adhesive. Foil tape over the joints of the panels helps stop thermal transfer.

Installing the SUBFLOOR and FINISH FLOORING

THE TERM *SUBFLOOR* refers to the foundation surface your decorative or finish flooring will go on top of. All homes need a subfloor, and so does your skoolie! The best material for a bus subfloor is sanded plywood. Oriented strand board, or OSB (another common subfloor material), is not the best option for a bus subfloor because it is more vulnerable to moisture and less resilient than sanded plywood.

Plywood subflooring should be at least ½ inch thick, but ⅝ inch and ¾ inch are better. If you have the budget and headroom, ⅝-inch or ¾-inch tongue-and-groove plywood subflooring is best because the pieces lock together so there's no movement along the panels' edges. You will trim the subfloor panels to fit the width of the bus, and it's all right to cut them a little short to make it easier to drop them into place on the floor. Sometimes thicker subflooring will not flex enough to drop below the bus's lower wall channel where one side of the seats rests, so trimming them an inch short helps. This will only leave a ½-inch gap along each wall, which will be disguised by the finish flooring. Just be sure the gaps are even on both sides to prevent the subfloor from being out of square, otherwise it's hard to align the next subfloor panel. You can always fill the ½-inch gaps with expanding spray foam after the subflooring is installed.

To secure the subfloor to the bus, I recommend using self-tapping, wood-to-metal screws to go through the subfloor and insulation and into the bus's metal floor (see Self-Tapping Screws on page 112). To guarantee a solid connection, the screws should be ½ inch longer than the total depth of the subfloor, the insulation, and the bus's metal floor. Note that these

To limit loss of headroom, you can use ½-inch plywood panels for the subfloor, but ⅝- or ¾-inch is preferable.

Cut the plywood to fit each section of the bus floor.

screws will create small thermal bridges for temperature outside the bus to travel into the bus, so don't go overboard on the number that you use. I have found that 9 to 12 screws work fine to secure each full-size subfloor panel. You can also use a foam-board adhesive between the subfloor and insulation boards to further ensure a solid connection.

Joining the subfloor panels together is a straightforward process: Lay the panel down beside the previous panel and push its edge flush against the other panel's edge. For added insurance, apply a bead of wood glue between the edges. Tongue-and-groove panels fit together just as their name suggests, and a bead of wood glue between the panels doesn't hurt.

While the self-tapping screws do an excellent job holding down the subfloor, if you're concerned that the floor is not secure enough, you can install baseboards along the sides of the bus. For baseboards, use 1×4 boards and fasten them to the walls with self-tapping screws.

Apply adhesive to the underside of the subfloor, if desired. This limits the number of screws required to secure the subfloor.

Screw the subfloor into the metal bus floor, using self-tapping screws that are long enough to go through the insulation.

The vinyl flooring we used snaps together. Vinyl is a durable, inexpensive option that comes in all sorts of styles.

A rubber mallet comes in handy, for gently tapping the pieces into place.

Another advantage of vinyl flooring is that it isn't too thick, which helps preserve headroom.

Be certain the baseboards are flat against the subfloor before screwing them in. Drive the screws into the side pillars, and drill pilot holes if the screws are stubborn about going in. *Never* use the outside skin of the bus as an attachment point. Only attach items to structural metal, not sheet metal!

The Finish Flooring

Finish flooring is the final layer you will walk on. Vinyl click-together, imitation-wood flooring works wonderfully for skoolies because it is extremely durable, relatively thin, and easy to install with great results. This style is considered a floating floor, meaning it doesn't have to be nailed or glued to the subfloor. Some vinyl flooring comes with an additional layer of padding on the underside to make the floor more comfortable. I've even used vinyl flooring on the walls!

Other types of flooring, such as carpet, laminate, and engineered hardwood, can also be laid right over the subfloor and are relatively easy to install. There are tons of flooring options, from cheap sheet vinyl to rubber tiles to reclaimed wood, but avoid using ceramic tile due to bus movement, engine vibrations, and potholes. It wouldn't take long for the tiles to come loose.

One good tip is to check the classifieds, online listings, or your local salvage store for leftover flooring from constructions jobs. You never know what you might stumble upon!

TINTING OR COVERING *Bus Windows*

Because bus windows allow so much temperature transfer, you might consider adding tinting film to them if they don't already have it. Window tint, or "window film," reduces temperature transfer through glass and is rated by a U-value, similar to insulation's R-value. Tinting windows yourself can be a time-consuming and persnickety task, but it can save you a lot of money over professional tinting. Alternatively, you can get an estimate from a professional tinting business and decide whether it's worth it.

If you decide to take on the task, get a reputable brand with film that has at least a 2-ply rating. Buying in bulk will save you money over car kits, even if you do end up with some material left over. Tints are rated by percentage of light that can pass through. For example, 5 percent "limo" tint is much darker than 20 percent. **Note:** Never tint a windshield or the front windows beyond the legal limit for your state!

The process begins with cleaning the window thoroughly. Next, mist the glass with water, then peel and stick the tinting film onto the window while using a flat squeegeelike tool to smooth out bubbles.

For windows that you don't need to see through, you can simply paint over them. Or you can apply a decorative window film, which installs just like window tint. Window film allows light to enter but provides privacy and can add a decorative touch (see photo below and on page 161). A third option is to remove unneeded bus windows and replace them with metal panels riveted or screwed into the window opening.

8

INTERIOR
FRAMING *and*
FINISHING

Now that your skoolie's subfloor is down and everything is insulated, you can move on to framing the interior according to your finalized layout plan. How much framing you do will depend on your layout and what you select for wall and ceiling finishes. Fortunately, the solid metal structure of a bus makes a great building framework, and the squareness of the walls minimizes the number of complicated cuts you have to make.

Taping off the layout of your bus interior will give you an idea of how your living space will flow and allow you a chance to do some fine-tuning.

Finalizing YOUR LAYOUT

IT'S TIME TO finalize your floor plan. First, it's smart to mock up the layout by using painter's tape or chalk to map it out on the empty subfloor. When you walk around the taped layer, if you feel something is too tight or if you find inefficiencies in how things are positioned, you can move the tape to test alternatives.

Make sure you've given yourself enough room to feel comfortable. Sure, you can attempt to fit everything into your bus, but maybe "everything" isn't as important as fitting in what makes you happy. If you want a shower in your bathroom but including one means you can fit only a full mattress in your sleeping area — and you can't sleep well on a full mattress — you'll have to pick one or the other. A quick shower outside your bus might be an easier pill to swallow than a bad night's sleep.

What about the kitchen area? Do you foresee four people eating at the table regularly, or will it be just you or you and a companion 95 percent of the time? A two-person booth instead of a large table can really open up floor space.

Relaxation space is important to prioritize as well. Do you find yourself watching TV or reading in bed more than you do from a sofa? If so, maybe your skoolie doesn't need a living room.

Are you nervous about not having enough storage space in your layout? It may help to make a list of everything you would move into your bus, then determine if those items will fit within your layout.

One of the most valuable lessons I've learned from designing skoolie layouts is to allow for an easily accessible space for all utilities to be installed (as well as incorporating wiring into your overall plan). Having to crawl under your bed to rewire a water pump is not a pleasant experience, which is why I suggest having a service wall or build-out that is easy to access (see page 117). Even if you have to give up a portion of your ideal layout, you will be thankful that you made that sacrifice when you go to inspect and maintain all the electrical and plumbing components.

Overall, it's best to base your layout on *your* personal preferences because you will be the one spending the most time there.

WALL *and* CEILING FRAMING

WALL FRAMING MAY involve attaching lumber to the existing bus walls to support decorative finish material. You also might want to build entirely new walls to partition the bus interior or wall off a small section for a bathroom or other private space.

Adding paneling or other finish material to wall framing is much like installing paneling in a house. Decorative finishes on bus ceilings are a little different. You can attach material directly to the ceiling framing using self-tapping screws (see Self-Tapping Screws on page 112). You can also run 1×4 planks from front to back along the ceiling of the bus to serve as attachment points for ceiling panels. Another option is to install 4-inch-wide strips of ½-inch plywood to the ceiling framing that runs from the left to the right side. The strips will bend to follow the curve of the roof and will serve as attachment points for your decorative ceiling, whether that's hardboard paneling or tongue-and-groove boards.

By using boards or plywood strips as attachment points, you reduce the number of screws going into the bus ceiling framing, which minimizes thermal bridging. You attach the finish materials with short screws that don't go all the way through the wood and into the metal roof. In any case, keep in mind that building out your ceiling with boards or plywood, plus the finish material, results in a modest loss of ceiling clearance; but every half inch counts on a skoolie!

Framing the Walls and Ceiling for Paneling

Framing the side walls of the bus for new paneling involves attaching vertical or horizontal boards to the sides of the bus with self-tapping screws. The paneling will fasten to this framing. If you want the walls to have vertical paneling, the framing boards must run horizontally. If the paneling will run horizontally, the framing must run vertically.

The standard technique for this framing is to use 1×4 boards and fasten them to the bus side supports with self-tapping screws. As described for ceiling framing, you can then install the wall finish with short screws that don't go all the way through the 1×4s. Alternatively, if you prefer to attach your wall panels directly to the bus side supports, be mindful of the number of self-tapping screws you use — to keep thermal bridging at a minimum.

We finished the interior walls of the bus with white wall paneling and rough-cut trim. Here, I'm framing in the wall for the utility room.

The reason I suggest using screws over nails for both framing and wall paneling is because a bus moves and vibrates. Nails are suitable for small trim, but they cannot match the holding strength of screws. Screws also have the ability to pull pieces together. For added insurance, exterior *construction-type* wood screws work best.

Before adding the wall paneling to the framing, take into account any electrical cable or water lines that will need to pass through the wall, running either perpendicular to or parallel with the wall studs. Use a ¾-inch drill bit or hole saw to make holes through the studs.

If you won't be covering one side of the wall (such as the back side of a back wall separating a "garage" space), you will have access to the studs from the back of the bus.

Framing New Walls

Framing partition walls in your bus can be done with 2×3 or 2×4 studs, but you save a little space with 2×3s without compromising much in stability, given that a bus ceiling is much shorter than a traditional house's ceiling (and therefore the walls are shorter). Before you install the studs, which run vertically, you

must install a horizontal board on the bottom for studs to attach to; this is known as a bottom plate. You also need a horizontal board at the top, called a top plate.

The bottom plate attaches to your subfloor with construction screws, and these should not exceed the depth of the subfloor. The top plate attaches to the ceiling with self-tapping screws. Make sure the top plate self-tapping screws go into the ceiling ribs and not the sheet metal. Or, if you are replacing the ceiling sheet metal, you can secure the top plate to the wood framing boards attached to the ceiling ribs.

MAKE SURE IT'S PLUMB! It is very important to make sure the bottom and top plates are in alignment so your wall is plumb, or perfectly vertical. However, because a bus isn't always sitting perfectly level, you will not be able to use a level to get an accurate reading for the interior framing. Here's the workaround: Attach the bottom plate first. Then, to locate the top plate accurately, use a full-size framing square, a straightedge (such as a straight board) tall enough to reach from floor to ceiling, a human helper, and a pencil or marker.

Stand up the framing square with its long leg facing toward the ceiling and the corner against one end of the bottom plate. Be sure that the short leg of the square is flush against the floor.

Have your helper hold the straightedge upright and flush with the long leg of the framing square from top to bottom, with no

SELF-TAPPING *Screws*

Self-tapping screws are installed just like a normal screw, but they have a drill-bit-like tip that is designed to drill into metal so that the screw essentially makes its own pilot hole. You'll need various sizes of self-tapping screws designed to attach wood to metal.

In my experience, even a self-tapping screw can struggle to get through the thick metal supports on a bus; predrilling the hole with a small metal-grade drill bit helps get the screw started.

gap between the straightedge and the square. Again, make sure the corner of the square is against the bottom plate and the short leg of the square is flush with the floor.

Use a pencil or marker to mark the ceiling along the top of the straightedge, thus transferring the location of the bottom plate to the ceiling. This mark notes the positioning of one side of the top plate. Repeat the same process to mark the opposite side of the bottom and top plates at both ends.

Now that you have your markers, you can install your top plate. Attach the plate with self-tapping screws going through the plate and into the bus ceiling framing. Don't worry about the top plate being at a slight angle — that angle will be met with the studs.

CURVE THE TOP END TO FIT THE CEILING. Because the top plate will attach to the curved ceiling, the top ends of the studs must be cut at an angle to fit flush against the top plate. To mark the angle for this cut, you can create a template with a piece of paper: Hold the paper against the ceiling and align one of its vertical edges with a fixed vertical edge in the bus (such as the rear door frame). Trace the angle of the top plate onto the paper with a pencil. Cut along the pencil line to create the template.

Determine the height of the wall stud, measuring from the bottom plate to the highest point on the top plate. Use the template to trace

Use a framing square — set parallel to the bottom plate — to make sure each stud is plumb side to side.

the angle of the top plate onto the stud, with the taller side of the template placed in the top corner of the stud.

Cut the stud and check its fit between the plates. Use a framing square to make sure the stud is plumb from side to side. If necessary, adjust the angle or recut the stud until it fits well. Use the cut stud as a template to trace the angle cut on the other studs. Fasten the studs

to the top and bottom plates with construction screws, driving the screws at an angle through the edges of the studs and into the plates — a technique known as toenailing. It helps to drill angled pilot holes for the screws.

As an alternative to using a top plate, you can secure the studs to the ceiling with metal L brackets, using two brackets per stud. Fasten the brackets with self-tapping screws driven

When framing in the walls, start drilling about an inch above the bottom plate to make sure the screw captures enough of both the stud and the plate.

into the ceiling framing (never through any thin metal, like the sheet metal on the bus walls and roof). These brackets do an excellent job of joining framework to bus walls, but it's a relatively expensive option compared to a 2×3 top plate.

Wall and Ceiling Finishes

As with flooring, nearly all wall and ceiling finish options available for houses also work in skoolies. When selecting finish materials for walls, review your layout to determine how much of the wall will be visible and how much will be covered by the bed, kitchen, woodstove flashing, or permanent furniture. Why spend

the time hanging fancy paneling if it will be covered up?

For a budget solution, walls and ceilings can be finished with deconstructed shipping

pallets, pieces of vinyl flooring, cheap 4×8-foot sheets of hardboard cut to size, tongue-and-groove boards, and much more.

Sabrina finished the wall of the utility room with rough-cut ash.

BUILDING A BED FRAME

THE STURDY METAL rail that runs along the lower wall on both sides (and is roughly a foot off the floor) makes for an excellent mounting surface for your bed frame. If your bed will run perpendicular to the bus walls, you can use 2×4s for the bed frame rails and mount them between the side rails of the bus. If you want a bed that runs parallel to the bus walls, you can mount 2×3 or 2×4 bed frame rails to one side of the bus directly on top of the metal rail along the lower part of the wall to support one side of the bed, and build a short wall that matches the height of the metal side rail to support the other side of the bed. In our bus, there is an interior partition wall next to the bed, so we installed a support rail on the wall to carry the interior ends of the bed rails.

If you want your bed to sit higher than the metal side rail, you can attach a 2×3 or 2×4 to the side of the bus with self-tapping screws going into the side supports; this creates a taller rail support for the bed frame rails to attach to. L brackets work well for attaching the bed frame rails directly to the side of the bus rail. Bed frame rails resting on a 2×3 or 2×4 can simply be secured with wood screws.

Our bed frame rests on rails attached to an interior wall, and will be finished with ½-inch plywood for the mattress to rest on. There's enough space below for a good amount of storage.

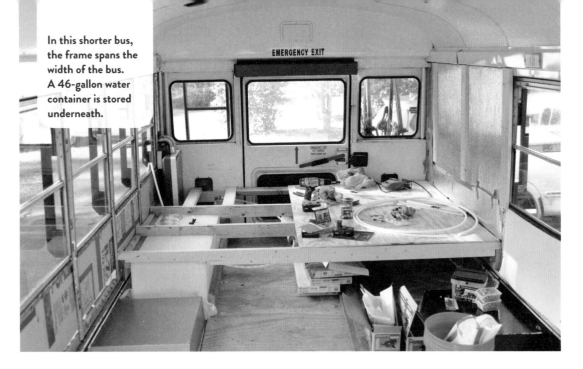

In this shorter bus, the frame spans the width of the bus. A 46-gallon water container is stored underneath.

Space the bed frame rails no more than 16 inches apart, and cover the rails with ½-inch plywood screwed down to create a flat surface for your mattress. You will need two 4×8-foot sheets of plywood to cover all bed frames that are larger than a twin.

If you want the bed to sit at a certain height to allow for maximum storage space underneath, be sure to take into account the height of the mattress you will use. Mattresses can range from 6 inches for a basic futon-style or memory foam mattress up to 16 inches or more for a pillow-top. So, for example, if you allow for 18 inches of clearance under your bed, then factor in 4 inches for the frame if you used 2×4s (a 2×4 actually measures 3½ inches wide, plus the ½-inch thickness of the plywood) and 14 inches for your mattress, you have a total height of 3 feet, leaving you with 3 to 3½ feet of space between the mattress and the ceiling.

The bed space is finished with ½-inch plywood. A water heater is installed in the leftover space at the foot of the bed, where the batteries will be housed, as well.

UTILITY AREAS. Depending on what kind of kitchen you'd like, or how elaborate you'd like the bathroom to be, you may need to do more framing. In our case, we used a reclaimed dresser as a kitchen sink vanity, so we didn't need to frame in the sink and a countertop. However, we did frame in a toilet closet for our bucket toilet, as well as a utility area at the back of the bus.

ENCLOSE THE WHEEL HUMPS. Framing around the wheel humps is straight-forward. Use 2×4s to square in the wheel hump and plywood to go over the 2×4s, creating a flat space. Be sure to insulate inside this "wheel box" to help minimize tire noise. Some people like to repurpose old insulation inside the wheel boxes, but new rigid insulation is much better. As with ceiling insulation, because the wheel humps are curved, you need to cut insulation boards into thin sections to wrap around the wheel well. Lots of seal tape can be used on the humps to seal the small gaps, and a can of expanding foam can work wonders for hard-to-reach locations.

TOM McCONNELL
BUS 'N' BREAKFAST
@BUSNBREAKFAST

Tom's skoolie is a Blue Bird 12-window-long flat-nose with a gorgeous interior! The driver's area is walled off from the rest of the bus, and a small "front door" opens to access the living space. When you walk in, there's a small classic Fisher woodstove on the right and a storage bench on the left. On the opposite end of the bus, the walled-off bedroom features a full bed *and* a full bathroom with toilet, sink base, and shower stall.

The kitchen counter is against the opposite side of the bedroom wall, and a large counter protrudes from the passenger-side wall just behind it. Two 100-watt solar panels are mounted to the roof for powering the lights and water pump.

The Bus 'n' Breakfast is an American school bus that now resides in Dorset, England. You can hire her out for events, like weddings or parties, or just for a weekend getaway.

9
skoolie KITCHENS

Many folks consider the kitchen to be the most important room in a home, and for good reason! A typical kitchen in a regular house includes counters and sink, upper and lower cabinets, table and chairs, and appliances. There's no reason you can't have these things in your skoolie, too, and in this chapter I'll explain how to make it all fit.

CABINETS *and* COUNTERTOPS

CABINETS AND COUNTERTOPS are the primary design elements of any kitchen space and usually determine a kitchen's overall size. For example, if you want a 6-foot-long counter mounted along the wall of your bus, that gives you a 45-square-foot kitchen area — the counter length multiplied by the width of the bus (7½ feet).

Countertop depth, measured from front to back, is largely determined by the depth of the base cabinets or shelving structure below. The depth of a standard kitchen counter is 25 inches, so a counter running along one wall leaves you with just under 5½ feet of kitchen floor space. Then again, there are no norms with skoolies, so why not look for another option and save some floor space?

One of my favorite skoolie hacks is to find a used bathroom vanity to repurpose as a kitchen cabinet. Many "comfort height" bathroom vanities are the same height as kitchen counters — at 36 inches, including the countertop — but are only 22 inches deep. That means you gain an extra 3 inches of floor space, and every inch counts in a tiny dwelling! Perhaps you will add those extra 3 inches to your table so there's enough space for guests.

> Open-faced cabinets cut down on weight and eliminate the concern of cabinet doors swinging open while you're driving or crowding the kitchen area when the doors are open. A small lip at the front of the cabinet opening will prevent items from sliding out.

Kitchen and bath cabinets can be found used or can be built from scratch. Yes, you can buy relatively inexpensive unfinished stock cabinets from a home center. But the fact is, used cabinets are easy to come by. Kitchen and bathroom remodeling is a favorite American pastime, and many homeowners and builders either donate perfectly good cabinets and vanities to building materials recyclers (which resell the items at bargain prices) or sell them online.

Another hack is to get used cabinets and cut the cabinet face frame from the box (the shelving portion). You can then install the face frame onto custom-built cabinet boxes or shelves, making the storage unit any depth you like, depending on how deep you want the counter.

For the countertop itself, you can build a custom surface or buy a prefab countertop and trim it to fit. Plastic laminate countertop sections are commonly sold at home centers and can be cut with a circular saw or jigsaw.

Regardless of what you use or build for cabinets and counters, keep in mind the size of the sink you'd like to use to make sure it fits inside the parameters of the counter.

Wall Cabinets

Wall, or above-the-counter, kitchen cabinets are challenging to fit and install because of the ceiling curve. Creating a template to represent the ceiling curve is helpful for trimming the backs

Overhead cabinets need to be cut to fit the curve of bus roof, which begins immediately over the windows.

of cabinets to fit, and you can hang them with an ample number of L brackets.

A great alternative to overhead cabinets is a shelving system with no cabinet doors. Each shelf has an outer ledge that keeps items from falling when the bus is on the move. Another popular idea is to take mason jars, attach the lids to the underside of a shelf with small wood screws, then store items inside the jars and simply screw each jar to its permanently secured lid. You can install L-shaped shelf

brackets between the window pillars and attach your shelf on top of them, or you can rest the back of your shelf above the windows and use small chains between the shelf edge and ceiling for support. Shelves weigh less than cabinets and are much more budget friendly.

There are endless options for building custom kitchen cabinets. Remember, you can keep the budget low if you scout for reclaimed materials.

KITCHEN APPLIANCES

BASIC KITCHEN APPLIANCES for a skoolie include a cooktop or oven and a refrigerator. A microwave, toaster, dishwasher, garbage disposal, and such are not commonly priorities. A microwave uses a ton of electricity, toasting can be done with an oven, and it's doubtful you'll have enough dishes in your tiny kitchen to justify a dishwasher!

Cooking

A variety of slide-in or drop-in cooktops are available online, but if you need an oven as well as a cooktop, Camp Chef sells an adorable camp oven with a stainless steel finish and in a nice small size. You can find old ovens removed from RVs, but be cautious of their condition.

The owners of this skoolie reclaimed a propane oven from an RV and retrofitted it into their kitchen. It's the perfect size for the space!

Nearly all of the suitable cooktop/oven options run on propane. Some use small disposable propane canisters but have the option to connect to a larger propane tank. Smaller camping stove burners sometimes use butane fuel. If you choose a large propane tank, do not store the tank inside the bus; keep it secured to the back or use a horizontal underbody tank. When using any gas-fueled cooking equipment, make sure the area is ventilated and your bus has a carbon monoxide detector (See Everyone: Get a CO Detector! on page 171).

Refrigeration

There's a refrigeration system for skoolie kitchens in every budget range. On the low end, a simple cooler or a fancy Yeti cooler functions well for part-time excursions, especially if you'd like to move the cooler in and out of your bus or bring it with you in another vehicle. The cons of a basic cooler are ice usage, melted ice that will need to be dumped, and space limitations. On the other hand, when you're traveling you can make it a habit to pick up a bag of ice whenever you fill up on fuel, then use the melted ice for rinsing water or pet water. Or you could buy a portable ice maker capable of making up to 26 pounds of ice in 24 hours and run it for a few hours using solar batteries or a power inverter connected to your alternator while driving. (Learn more about solar batteries and power inverters in chapter 11.)

There are 12-volt powered coolers available that don't need ice and can run directly off solar batteries. The manufacturers Dometic and ARB carry lines of powered coolers that can consume less than 1 amp-hour per hour. Although these brands are costly, they are considered to be a one-time investment because of their durability. Less expensive powered coolers, such as models from Koolatron, are available, too.

A traditional upright refrigerator will take up more space than a cooler but may suit you if space allows and extra capacity is necessary. You can power this type of refrigerator with a power inverter, but don't skimp on the inverter because it will operate full time, and you don't want to wake up to a refrigerator full of spoiled food. A 7½-cubic-foot apartment-size refrigerator, for instance, can consume 75 or more amp-hours per day. Compare that power usage to the 12-volt coolers mentioned above.

Be sure to secure your refrigerator to your bus! Large L brackets between the fridge and bus wall supports and floor work well. Be careful: don't use a screw that is so long that it punctures the inside wall of the refrigerator when attaching the L bracket. I suggest using two L brackets attached to the wall and two on the floor.

A propane Camp Chef oven fits perfectly alongside our dresser, repurposed as a kitchen base cabinet.

KITCHEN TABLE *Ideas*

Kitchen table booth seats can double as passenger seating while your skoolie is on the move, or the table can be attached to the wall with hinges so it can fold out of the way to add floor space when needed. In any case, it's smart to attach your kitchen table to the bus wall to keep it secured.

Many folks like to build booth-style seating for their tables that also have storage underneath the seats.

Another great kitchen hack is to repurpose two of the original bus seats as seating at the kitchen table. Two bus seats, one from each side of the bus, can be turned to face each other and spaced any desired distance apart. You can secure these seats to the bus floor in the same fashion as they were originally, but use new bolts that can pass through the extra floor thickness.

The side of the seat that is against the window can be reattached to the lower wall side rail; however, you will need to add a piece of wood on top of the wall rail to compensate for the extra floor thickness. You can also repurpose the bus seat cushions by themselves to use as booth cushions.

Two of the orginal bus bench seats work perfectly with a table booth!

It's nice to keep a small folding table on board, to set up an outdoor cooking area for festivals and trips with friends. This also limits traffic in and out of your skoolie.

OUTDOOR *Kitchens*

OUTDOOR KITCHENS ARE a great way to escape the confines of your skoolie! Why cook inside on a beautiful day, especially when you have the ability to drive your home to beautiful locations? A small barbecue grill can be stowed under your bed or in an underbody storage box and pulled out with ease for use on nice days.

Van lifers often use heavy-duty drawer sliders to roll a kitchen counter in and out of the back of their rigs, but the back of a school bus usually sits too high up to provide a comfortable working surface. Your options are to build a fold-up table on the side of your bus or to store a folding table inside your bus for occasional use. Easy setup is a top priority for any mobile outdoor kitchen; keeping its function simple will make for a more enjoyable experience.

ROBIN SCHANNEP AND FAMILY

CONTENTED NOMADS

@CONTENTEDNOMADS

The Contented Nomads bus is a 1997 International flat-nose occupied by a family of six plus a dog! The family, based on the West Coast, has lived full-time in their bus for nearly 3 years. They love being able to make a home wherever they park, whether that's in the woods or by the beach.

The bus is 37 feet long and uses solar and propane as well as a standard electrical hookup cable when electricity is available. A 35-gallon tank provides water. The bus bathroom features a composting toilet and a large, round metal tub for a shower and bathtub.

courage, dear heart.

SCHANNEP FAMILY
CONTENTED NOMADS

There are two sets of bunk beds for the kids and a large L-shaped sofa in the front of the bus. The kitchen includes counter space on both sides of the bus, with an apartment-size oven and refrigerator on one side and a double sink on the other. In the rear of the bus is a large bedroom with an overhead bookshelf.

10 *skoolie* BATHROOMS

When nature calls, having a private space is a given in any home, but how much effort — and space — should you devote to your mobile comfort station? A skoolie bathroom can be anything from a tiny, curtained toilet alcove to a full bath with a comfy toilet, a sink, and a shower (or even a soaking tub!). You might take some functions outside the walls, with an outdoor shower or a portable toilet. It all depends on your personal priorities and how you envision your everyday life in a school bus.

BATHROOM
Options

THE SPACE YOU allot for a bathroom will understandably depend on how much overall space you have available, but finding the right balance between your private needs and your living space is a more personal decision. Perhaps you're the type of person who absolutely must have a morning shower, or maybe you're more comfortable with a shower every few days. Maybe you are terrified of public restrooms or of doing your business outdoors, or maybe you are fine carrying a simple emergency "head" just for urgent situations. Bathroom solutions exist for all budgets; just understand that there will likely be compromises to make, as with any off-grid, tiny-living lifestyle.

Toilets on the Go

If you have other showering plans, such as an outdoor setup or a campground or rest-stop shower, you can save space by having only a toilet inside your skoolie. A portable toilet can be stowed away and pulled out when needed, or you can designate a small space of your bus for the toilet to be permanently installed. A toilet room can be as narrow as one side window of your bus. You can wall around the toilet for privacy or simply curtain off the area. Assuming

> A platform built around a 5-gallon bucket allows for any standard toilet seat to be installed. Toilet odors can be eliminated by adding wood chips before and after your toilet-business is finished.

you have a kitchen sink, you can eliminate the sink from the bathroom and use the kitchen sink for washing hands and brushing teeth.

Skoolie toilet options range from inexpensive portable camping units sold at ordinary big box stores, to permanent composting toilets that can cost nearly ten times as much, to DIY units that work surprisingly well and cost next to nothing. Each option has its own system to minimize odor.

BASIC PORTABLE TOILETS have two sections: one for the toilet lid and bowl and the other for the waste. There is also a small fluid reservoir that releases a small amount of liquid deodorizer into the toilet bowl when "flushing." Basic portable toilets can be emptied at an RV dump station.

COMPOSTING TOILETS allow moisture to evaporate from waste, leaving only compost that is easy to empty. A composting toilet vents the odor out of the bus and has a drawer on the bottom of the toilet for removing and emptying the composted waste. The toilet will slowly turn the waste to make the liquid evaporate faster.

DIY COMPOSTING TOILETS come in many shapes and sizes — and the price is right. It may sound harsh, but it's entirely possible to use a simple 5-gallon bucket as a toilet. You can box in the bucket with wood and install a hinged lid on top of the bucket that has a hole cut out for sitting over. To add comfort, you can install an actual toilet seat lid on top of the wood box lid. It will feel just like home!

DIY composting toilets use sawdust or wood chips to cover the smell. You first put down a layer of sawdust to cover the bottom of the bucket, then you completely cover the waste with sawdust or chips each time you use the toilet. (Save sawdust during your skoolie conversion. When it runs out, you can buy sawdust by the bag.) A DIY toilet can be emptied into a composting bin that will break down the waste into a fertilizer for nonfood use. I prefer to line my bucket throne with environmentally friendly, biodegradable portable toilet bags that can be sealed and delivered to a compost bin with minimal hassle. These bags greatly simplify disposal.

If you want to get fancier with your DIY toilet, install urine diverters or separators (available online) that will route your pee to a separate container that you empty at a different time than your solid waste. Keeping the two elements separated helps reduce odor.

Regardless of how you set up a toilet for life on the road, you will have to deal with the waste at some point. If you have a blackwater tank (more on these in chapter 13) that holds all your waste, you still need to empty it eventually. Trust me: it's not a pleasant task! Emptying a smaller quantity more regularly is much less unpleasant, in my opinion.

If you have the room in your budget, an electric composting toilet is a turnkey solution.

SHOWERS *and* TUBS

SKOOLIE SHOWERS OR tubs come in many shapes and sizes. Some folks like to use a large steel stock tank (sold at farm supply stores) for bathing or showering. Others install conventional tubs or shower stalls. In any case, remember that you'll need a graywater tank for your indoor shower or tub to drain into (see chapter 13). I suggest using a showerhead that has a pause button to conserve water.

Showers can be built by custom-cutting shower wall panels in combination with a shower base. Shower bases come in many sizes, with 30 × 30 inches being the smallest available. A mop sink can be retrofitted as a tiny shower stall if you're willing to squeeze inside a 2 × 2-foot space. Or look around for a used RV shower base or complete shower insert. RV showers and tubs also can be purchased new.

If you prefer a natural material for the bathroom walls and trim, cedar is best for a shower area because it can handle moisture better than other common softwoods.

Ventilation

Bathrooms with showers or tubs should include a vent fan to remove the steamy air. This can be accomplished with a small window fan in the bathroom area, or you might rely on a roof fan in the common ceiling area of the bus. Simply cracking a window open while showering will ventilate moisture as well.

A stock tank can be used as a bathtub! Both oval and round tanks are sold at farm supply stores in a variety of sizes. This bathing area is wrapped in cedar paneling and is separated from the rest of the skoolie by a solid wall.

Outdoor SHOWERS

Outdoor showers don't take up any space inside the skoolie, and they don't require additional plumbing! Setup time can be a downside of using an outdoor shower, as can bad-weather days when you will have to brave the elements and the cold. But you're living in a school bus; you can handle the elements from time to time, right?!

An outdoor shower can use water lines running either to the outside (for an outdoor connection) or to the back door (which you open to access the water lines). Another option is a portable tankless all-in-one water heater and pump (see page 184). Or you could use a hanging shower bag or DIY CPVC-pipe hot-water rig to heat and gravity-feed your shower water. Whichever method you select, I personally recommend utilizing the bus door as part of the shower privacy strategy.

To outfit the outdoor shower, bend a long piece of ½-inch or ¾-inch PVC pipe (PEX will work, too) to create a rounded curtain rod, then hang a couple standard shower curtains from the rod. You could also make a square rod using PVC elbows. To make the curtain rod removable, use plumbing flanges that are mounted permanently to the bus (with caulk and self-tapping screws), then simply stick the ends of the curtain rod into the flanges when it's time to shower. For the shower floor, a cedar shower platform is perfect; you can buy one premade or build your own. Remember to use environmentally friendly soaps for your outdoor shower!

A propane point-of-use water heater uses a minimal amount of electricity and provides plenty of hot water from a standard grill-size propane tank.

WILL WINKELMAN'S
VINTAGE SKOOLIE

AT THE OTHER END OF THE SPECTRUM from the homebuilt, DIY skoolie is this 1959 Chevrolet Viking that was re-envisioned by Portland, Maine–based architect Will Winkelman and restored by his team of builders and mechanics. The client saw the abandoned bus in a field and wanted to turn it into a guest space for his family's camp, as well as a fun vehicle for road trips.

WILL WINKELMAN'S
VINTAGE SKOOLIE

The lengthy restoration process involved rebuilding the vehicle from the chassis up, to make it roadworthy, then designing and building the interior. The bus can seat 13 passengers with seat belts when it's in motion and can sleep two people — either in separate twin beds or one queen, when the twins are joined.

⑪ OFF-GRID *power*

Part of the excitement of owning a skoolie is the freedom from being tied to one location. But if your only source of electricity is an extension cord running to a house outlet, then you are still tethered to the grid! In this chapter, we'll explore a few alternative power solutions that can help you whisk your skoolie into power independence. All these options will require more research based on your bus's electrical system and your specific power needs, but this overview will get you started.

POWER BASICS

THERE ARE THREE standard options for providing power to a skoolie: a gas generator, batteries charged by your bus's engine, and a solar photovoltaic system. We'll discuss each of these in more detail in this chapter. Regardless of the power source, most skoolies get their "house" electricity through 12-volt power systems.

Just about every motorized vehicle, including a bus, uses a 12-volt, direct current (DC) electrical system for power distribution through the vehicle. A 12-volt system is powered by a large battery (or battery bank) charged by a vehicle's alternator, by a generator, or via solar panels. The 12-volt power is distributed through low-voltage wiring from the battery to various electrical devices such as lights, speakers, and power outlets. Most connections are not made directly to the battery; instead, the wiring connects to a fuse box that handles the power distribution and protects each branch with a fuse.

Since RVs and boats use 12-volt systems, there's a big market for 12-volt devices, wiring, and other components. This means you can find almost anything you need — from lights to fans to water pumps — in a 12-volt version. For any remaining appliances or devices that require standard household power, which is 120-volt alternating current (AC) electricity, you can wire a power converter to your battery and plug the appliance into the converter, just like a regular household electrical outlet.

Regardless of the type of off-grid power source you've chosen — whether it's solar, a generator, an additional battery connected to the bus alternator, or a combination of these — you will always use batteries to store your power.

How Much Power Do You Need?

The first step in planning your off-grid system is to determine how much power you need. Add up the wattage rating (watts) of each device you expect to use in your skoolie daily — such as lights, computers, phones, and kitchen appliances — then plug that total figure into a free off-grid calculator found online. Be sure to select "12 volt" if the calculator has options or a blank space for typing in the battery bank voltage. As a general example, a medium-size bus with eight lights, a water pump, two USB jacks, a 12-volt cooler, and an inverter that is used 4 minutes a day to power a travel-size hair dryer will require up to 1,000 watt-hours per day.

When calculating your power needs, the total wattage is the rate at which your devices consume energy, while the watt-hours represent the total usage; that is, how many watts you use over time. For example, a 1,200-watt hair dryer used for an entire hour will consume 1,200 watt-hours of energy. If you use that hair dryer only for 5 minutes, you will divide 5 by 60 (the number of minutes in an hour), then multiply the result by the dryer's wattage rating (1,200):

5 minutes of use ÷ 60 minutes = 0.08

0.08 × 1,200 watts = 96 watt-hours used in that 5-minute period

Keep in mind that the hair dryer still uses 1,200 watts of power to run for any length of time, so the inverter you plug it into must be rated for at least 1,200 watts (a hair dryer is one of those household items you would plug into an inverter; it needs too much power for a 12-volt system). If you can't find the wattage rating on a device, you can multiply its voltage (volts) rating by its amperage (amps) rating:

volts × amps = watts.

Because of the number of watt-hours a house (on wheels or otherwise) uses in a day, electrical specifications and amounts of usage are often given in kilowatt-hours, or kWh. One kWh is equal to 1,000 watt-hours. To convert your watt-hours total to kWh, simply divide the watt-hours by 1,000. For example, 1,300 watt-hours is equal to 1.3 kWh.

Play around with the online calculator to get a sense of how much power you will need to live comfortably in your skoolie. This may require you to spend more money than you had anticipated, so be prepared to compromise on your energy consumption by making some reductions. Rest assured, though, you can always add on to your off-grid system if your power needs grow.

GAS GENERATORS

PORTABLE GAS GENERATORS are rated in watts of output and usually have a "surge" or "peak" wattage rating that is available only for a short time of power use. The "running watts" rating is what you will base your selection on, and it's wise to have more running watts available for use rather than just enough.

To use a generator as your primary source of power, either you will have to stick with standard household 110/120-volt AC devices, or you will have to use the generator to charge a battery (or battery bank) for your 12-volt devices. If for some reason you have only 12-volt items and no battery setup, you can find AC-to-DC converters that plug into your generator to convert the 120-volt outlet on the generator to a cigarette-style 12-volt outlet. But if the generator is your only source of power, it's best to have a 12-volt system powered by batteries for your lights and other electronics, while keeping the batteries charged with the generator.

An inverter-type generator is the best choice for this because of its clean, level power output that will protect your batteries. Inverter generators usually come with battery cables specifically for charging house batteries. If

Gas-powered inverter generators are a quick and easy way to provide electricity to your skoolie. Mounting one to a rear platform or bracket makes access easy and keeps exhaust fumes behind the bus.

your skoolie uses a solar system, an inverter generator comes in handy on those stretches of cloudy days when your solar system needs some help meeting your power needs.

Small generators sometimes have a two-cycle engine that requires premixed gas-and-oil fuel, similar to the engines used in weed trimmers and chainsaws. These tend to be loud and can be hard to start, and they typically pollute more than larger engines. They can power a radio and TV while tailgating but tend to be underpowered for much more than that.

Larger generators have four-cycle gas engines similar to those in push lawnmowers. These use regular gas, rather than a gas-oil mixture, but be sure to read the owner's manual in case the engine requires non- or low-ethanol gas. Four-cycle engines are generally quieter, more powerful, cleaner-burning, and more reliable than two-cycle engines.

Inverter generators are excellent for use with delicate electronics because they produce clean, pure sine wave power. By "clean" power, I mean consistent power. A *pure sine wave* inverter generator maintains a steadier amplitude than a regular, *modified sine wave* generator, minimizing power fluctuations that can damage sensitive electronics. Inverter generators typically have stylish, hard-plastic casings with easy-to-grip handles, and they tend to run quieter than conventional generators, which consist of an exposed engine and alternator surrounded by a metal cage. The disadvantage of many inverter generators is the lack of an oil filter: you will have to change the generator's oil every 12 to 15 hours of use.

Bus ENGINE POWER

USING YOUR BUS engine for electricity is another option. The engine can provide power used while traveling, and it can charge house batteries used when you're parked. That said, I do not recommend using the existing engine batteries for power in your skoolie! At most, I suggest connecting a small-wattage battery-power inverter to one of the bus engine's batteries that will be used *only* while the bus is running and *never* when it's shut off. Your bus's engine batteries need to have all available cold-cranking amps to start the engine; placing any other power load on them could draw them down so the bus won't start.

What's the best way to use the bus engine for electricity? Add house batteries inside your skoolie that are charged while you're driving your bus. Essentially, the batteries are stored in a location that works with your bus layout and that provides easy to access for running 14- or 16-gauge electrical cable to 12-volt accessories.

AGM-type (adsorbed glass mat) batteries, used with solar systems, are ideal for this setup because they can safely be installed in tight interior spaces without needing to be vented (see Batteries for Power Storage on page 156). The AGM batteries will get their charge from the bus's engine battery or directly from the bus's alternator, which is bolted to the front of the engine.

The bus alternator has a pulley that is rotated by the serpentine belt to turn the alternator along with the engine. The alternator generates electricity to recharge the bus engine battery when the engine is running. Alternators have a positive terminal where a new cable of at least 12-gauge (wires get thicker as the gauge numbers get smaller) can be attached and routed through the wall between the engine compartment and the cab area, known as the firewall. Various black rubber plugs on the firewall allow wires to pass into the cab from the engine compartment, and you can route the new power cable through one of these plugs.

You can also connect this power cable to the positive terminal on one of the bus engine's batteries (assuming your bus has two batteries; either battery will work). Be sure to use heavy-duty copper battery lugs to connect the power wire to the positive post on either the engine battery or the alternator.

To protect the battery and alternator, you must install an in-line 30-amp circuit breaker (a car audio circuit breaker works great) near the beginning of the power cable in a spot that is easy to access. Install a second circuit breaker at the opposite end of the power cable, just before the new house batteries.

Next, you need a switch for connecting and disconnecting the house batteries from the engine battery or alternator. You turn this switch on to charge the batteries when the bus engine is running, and you turn it off when the engine is off. This prevents the house batteries from drawing power from the bus engine batteries, which could leave you stranded! The switch can be a basic knife-blade switch or a fancier one with a knob. Another option is to use a heavy-duty battery isolator that automatically prevents current from running both directions and draining the engine batteries.

Finally, you must ground the house batteries to the bus's frame. Use 4-gauge or larger grounding wire and a copper battery lug to connect the ground to an existing frame bolt, such as one of the bolts holding the rear bumper to the bus frame. You now have house batteries that can be connected to a 12-volt fuse box holder where all your 12-volt accessories will connect. If desired, you can connect a battery level indicator to the house batteries for monitoring their charge level.

Remember: Don't forget to disconnect the switch between the house batteries and the engine battery when the engine is off!

SOLAR POWER

OVERALL, I HIGHLY recommend solar power for your skoolie. Solar power has come a long way technology-wise, and the cost of parts has dropped a lot in the last decade. Even though the setup process may sound complicated, it's worth the headache. (And it would be a shame not to take advantage of the ample roof space of your skoolie for solar panels!) There's nothing like the feeling you get when you wake each morning and see your batteries charging with the sun.

There's ample space on bus roofs for solar panels. If you can't afford all the panels you need at first, it's easy to add more to the existing panels' wiring later on.

Solar System Elements

Off-grid solar photovoltaic (PV) systems consist of solar panels (a group of panels is called an array), a charge controller, and a battery bank. The charge controller controls and monitors the electrical power coming in from the array and delivers it to the batteries. The batteries supply all of the power to the bus's house system.

Solar panels and batteries provide DC power. All 12-volt (DC) wiring for the skoolie can be fed by a fuse block that connects to the batteries. If 120-volt AC power is required (for standard household devices), you can connect a DC-to-AC power inverter to the batteries and plug the devices into the inverter.

How Many Solar Panels Do You Need?

Let's say you've done the math and have determined you will use 1,500 total watt-hours (1.5 kWh) per day, and you want to be fully reliant on solar panels for power. How many panels will you need? Well, that depends on how much sunlight you get! You can find the peak sun hours for your location using a solar map found online, then plug that figure into a solar panel calculator along with your watt-hours figure to determine how many solar panels you need. For example, at 1,500 watt-hours of energy consumption per day in the Mid-Atlantic region the United States, you will need two 300-watt panels, or six 100-watt panels.

Choosing and Installing Solar Panels

The most common types of solar panels are rigid panels made with either monocrystalline or polycrystalline ("mono" and "poly" for short) solar cells. Monocrystalline panels are considered to be more efficient because they take less space to generate the same output as polycrystalline panels, and they have a longer life expectancy, but they cost slightly more. (With solar panels, "efficiency" refers to how much sunlight gets converted to electricity; greater efficiency is better.) For a skoolie, it makes sense to get as much efficiency out of your panels as possible, but rest assured that either style panel will suit your needs.

Solar panels come in various sizes that typically range from 50 to 300 watts. The 100-watt panels are popular for school bus conversions because they fit easily on either side of the roof and they're not as costly as a 300-watt panel. Many folks like to gradually add to their solar systems as funding becomes available, so the 100-watt panels make an excellent starting point.

Mounting the solar panels on your roof can be as straightforward or complex as you'd like. Solar panel mounting kits include brackets that attach to your bus's roof with self-tapping screws. Be sure to apply outdoor-grade silicone caulk between the brackets and the roof to prevent leaks.

If you want to get fancy and use your panels to their full potential, you can install them so that they can be tilted to face the sun. There's no standard way of tilting panels, so feel free to get creative. One method is to add heavy-duty door hinges to one side of a panel and use wingnuts to make it easy to disconnect the panel from a bracket on the other side; once the panel is disconnected on the bracket side, it can be tilted. You might use boards to hold the panels in their tilted position, or you could install small trunk struts between the panel and the nonhinged bracket.

Remember: Angle the panels only when your bus is parked; don't drive with the panels tilted up!

Personally, I like my panels to be as secure as possible and haven't felt the need to make them tiltable. But I do like having the ability to walk between my panels to clean them from time to time. I installed a 2×10 pressure-treated board down the center of my roof to use as a super-solid walking plank. If you go this route, you can attach the plank to the roof with self-tapping screws, but be sure to put a piece of plastic between the wood and the bus roof to prevent the pressure-treatment chemicals in the wood from corroding the bus roof (a piece of 6-mil plastic sheeting works great).

Charge Controllers

A solar charge controller is the next element in line after your panels are selected. The charge controller basically converts the energy collected by the panels into a voltage that can charge batteries. There are two basic types of charge controllers: pulse width modulated (PWM) and maximum power point tracking (MPPT). PWM types tend to be the cheapest and are better suited for smaller, more basic solar systems, but they are less efficient, so they lose a little more energy in the conversion process. MPPT controllers are more expensive and efficient, but they perform best in larger solar setups of 400 watts or more.

Solar kits for small, simple systems usually come with PWM charge controllers, and these are fine in most circumstances. But if you desire more power efficiency and can afford a MPPT controller, then by all means go for it! Also, the more expensive controllers display information that helps you monitor your system. Most MPPT controllers offer real-time data of the incoming and outgoing voltage and amps, and some even have data ports so that you can connect and mount a secondary monitor somewhere inside your skoolie for easy viewing. If you plan to increase the size of your solar array in the near future, it makes sense to invest in an MPPT controller up front.

Efficiency in charge controllers is judged by how well they manage incoming solar power. An MPPT controller converts excess voltage into charging amps, which is why it is more efficient than the PWM models, which don't convert excess voltage. If you need 300 or fewer watts from a solar system, and you don't expect to expand the system later, a PWM charger will work fine for your needs. On the other hand, if you are starting out with even a small, 100-watt solar system but plan to add panels in the immediate future, investing in an MPPT controller now will further motivate you to add on to your system.

Aside from these two types, charge controllers are offered in different sizes based on their amperage rating. The size of your panels' total wattage and the voltage you use for your system

Solar panels can be mounted with basic angle brackets, self-tapping screws and caulking found at your hardware store, or you can order brackets specifically designed for your panels.

Reserving a spot for a utility area that's easy to access is important. This utility room holds the solar charge controller, power inverter, battery, wiring, water tank, water pump, and water heater. This door previously opened for a wheelchair lift.

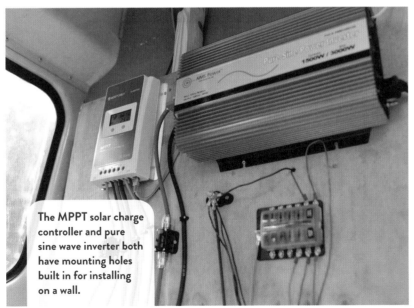

The MPPT solar charge controller and pure sine wave inverter both have mounting holes built in for installing on a wall.

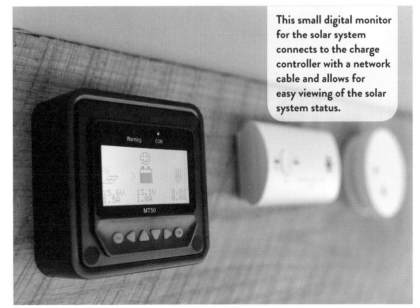

This small digital monitor for the solar system connects to the charge controller with a network cable and allows for easy viewing of the solar system status.

(assuming 12 volts) determine how large of a controller you need. For instance, a common 30-amp (30A) controller in a 12-volt system can handle 360 watts (30 amps × 12 volts = 360 watts) of output from the solar panels.

If you have six 100-watt panels, then you would need a 50-amp controller capable of handling 600 watts in a 12-volt system (600 watts ÷ 12 volts = 50 amps). Alternatively, you could wire your batteries in a 24-volt configuration, so that 600 watts of power divided by 24 volts would require only a 25-amp charge controller. But for the sake of simplicity, let's focus on 12-volt systems.

Parallel vs. Series Configuration

Parallel and series are two different wiring configurations for connecting two or more solar panels together to end up with a single set of wires going into the charge controller. In a parallel system, the positive and negative of each panel combine into one set of positive and negative cables that connect to the charge controller. In a series system, the positive from one panel connects to the negative of the next panel; to connect the array (group of panels), the first panel's negative connects to the charge controller and the last panel's positive connects to the charge controller.

Each wiring configuration has a different effect on the amperage and voltage of the array. With parallel wiring, you add up the amperage of all of the panels, while the voltage stays the same. For example, two 12-volt, 7-amp panels wired in parallel will equal 14 amps at 12 volts. Conversely, if you connect the same panels with series wiring, the voltages of the panels add together while the amperage stays the same as a single panel, so you would have 7 amps total at 24 volts. In both cases, you have the same total wattage (remember that volts × amps = watts):

Parallel: 12 volts × 14 amps = 168 watts

Series: 24 volts × 7 amps = 168 watts

Determining the best wiring configuration for your solar system depends on the type of charge controller you will use and the size of your solar panel array.

MPPT charge controllers maximize the efficiency of your panels when they are wired in series, resulting in the highest voltage. Just be sure to check the controller's specific limits for voltage before connecting the panels. If the panels will exceed the voltage limit, you will have to wire the panels in parallel.

PWM charge controllers are best suited for solar panels wired in parallel because any excess voltage that would come from wiring the panels in series would be lost due to the voltage limits of the PWM controller.

If you plan to add to your PV array in the near future, calculate the planned increase in voltage and determine whether or not your controller can handle it. If it can't handle the added voltage, it is best to stick with a parallel configuration.

WANT TO BE *Flexible?*

As an alternative to standard rigid solar panels, flexible panels are available that can be attached to your roof with heavy-duty roof seal tape used for RVs. Flexible solar panels can conform to the curve of the bus's roof, lessening the possibility of the panels catching low-hanging branches, and they don't interrupt the sleekness of a bus's roof. On the flip side, flexible panels cannot be tilted to point the panels toward the sun, and they typically offer much lower efficiency than rigid panels.

Solar System Wiring

Now that you've decided between wiring your solar panels in parallel or series, you are ready to route the wires into the controller. Solar panel cables connect using MC4 connectors that come pre-attached to the panels. MC4 connectors have male or female ends that are very easy to connect. The cables from the solar panels are usually less than 2 feet long, so you may need to purchase extension cables to reach the charge controller unless extensions were included with the panels.

To wire multiple panels in parallel, you must use MC4 "Y" adapters to combine the pair of positive and negative wires from each panel to make a single pair of positive and negative cables to connect into the charge controller in the bus. The total number of panels you can wire to the charge controller will depend on how many amps it is designed to handle. A 30-amp charge controller can handle four 7-amp panels.

If you connect the panels in series, you won't need MC4 "Y" adapters, and only the first and last panel in the array will connect to the charge controller.

In either case, if the panels or adapters that connect to the charge controller are some distance from the controller, you will need extra PV cables with an MC4 connector on one end to make the "home runs" from the panel cables to the controller. The end with the MC4

Solar panels have two cables, positive and negative, with MC4 connectors. Multiple panels can be connected with Y adapters.

Solar wires must enter the bus interior somehow! A one-inch drill bit makes a hole large enough for the two wires to fit through. Gently insert the cables through the hole to prevent the metal roof from cutting into them.

A solar double-cable "entry gland" works perfectly to seal around the solar cables where they enter the bus.

connector connects to the panel lead, while the other end of the home run cable connects directly to the charge controller without an MC4 connector.

Creating a custom-length solar cable is easy and is somewhat like adding a new plug to an extension cord. Start with PV cable (sold in 50-foot lengths; sometimes called PV wire) and MC4 connectors that match the original wiring on the panels. Cut the cable to the desired length, then strip the cable end. Unscrew the MC4 connector, slide it over the stripped cable

end, and screw the MC4 adapter back together to secure it. You can do the same at the other end of the cable (if you need MC4 connectors at both ends) or leave the cable bare to connect to the charge controller.

The ideal way to get the solar wiring through the roof and into the bus is through a part called a weatherproof solar cable entry gland or a solar cable entry housing. To mount this part, you first drill a hole through the roof large enough to fit a ½-inch PVC pipe or PEX tubing (a 4-inch length works perfectly). Add caulking

to the outside of the tube and around it on the roof. This will act as a protective tunnel so that no sharp metal edges harm your cables. Because solar charge controllers don't use MC4 connectors, the hole needs to be just large enough for the cables coming into the bus from the panels on the roof will simply be stripped on the end. The gland/housing will fit over the cable-entry hole and attach to the bus roof with self-tapping screws and silicone caulk. The gland/housing will come with the necessary parts to make a tight seal around the cables as they pass through.

Once the solar panels and batteries are wired to the charge controller, you are ready to distribute the power. A 12-volt fuse block wired to the battery bank makes it easy to connect wires for your lights and other small 12-volt devices, and the wiring and devices will be protected by fuses. Again, items that use a standard 120-volt house plug will require a power inverter.

As with inverter-type gas generators (page 147), there are modified sine wave inverters and pure sine wave inverters, with the latter being more costly but necessary for protecting delicate electronics. Most devices will be fine with a modified sine wave power inverter, but the pure sine wave versions eliminate the risk of ruining your devices. Follow the manufacturer's specifications for wiring an inverter to the battery bank.

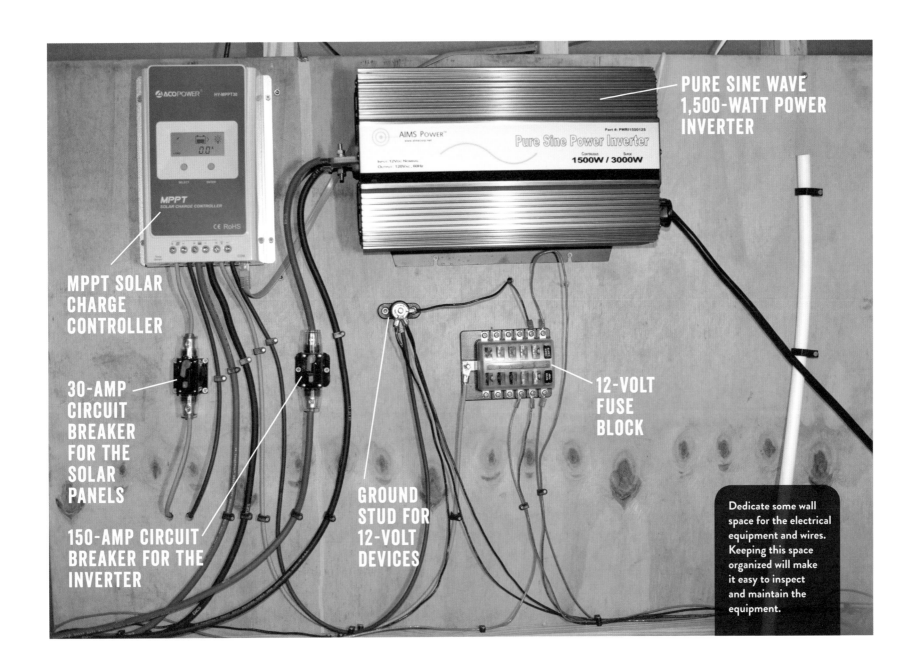

PURE SINE WAVE 1,500-WATT POWER INVERTER

MPPT SOLAR CHARGE CONTROLLER

30-AMP CIRCUIT BREAKER FOR THE SOLAR PANELS

150-AMP CIRCUIT BREAKER FOR THE INVERTER

GROUND STUD FOR 12-VOLT DEVICES

12-VOLT FUSE BLOCK

Dedicate some wall space for the electrical equipment and wires. Keeping this space organized will make it easy to inspect and maintain the equipment.

WIRE GAUGE AND FUSES

It's wise to include an in-line MC4 fuse between the panels and the charge controller. The charge controller has six wire slots for connecting the positive and negative wires from the panels to the controller, from the controller to the batteries, and from the controller to a 12-volt fuse box. In-line fuses should be installed on all positive cables to protect against damage to the equipment.

If your system includes a power inverter, it will connect directly to one of the sets of terminals in the battery bank; the positive wire from this connection should include an in-line fuse that matches the amp rating of the inverter.

The wires in and out of the charge controller can range from 8- to 10-gauge from the solar panels and 4- to 6-gauge to the battery. Be sure to use copper lugs for the cable ends, and do not leave any wire showing. Heat-shrink cable tubing will help cover any exposed copper wire, including the small tip that gets pinched inside the end of the copper lugs. Copper lugs perform best and can be used for all wire connections.

The wire gauge going from the battery to the power inverter is determined by the distance between the inverter and the battery: the longer the distance, the thicker the wire; 2- to 4-gauge wire is a safe range.

Batteries for Power Storage

Choosing batteries for your off-grid system is more complicated than buying a new battery for your car. First, your car battery is rated by cold-cranking amps (CCA), meaning its power is designed for frequent short draws rather than longer-term, slow discharge. The right type of battery for a solar system — and for storing power from a generator or bus alternator — is a deep-cycle battery. And if you plan to have your batteries inside your bus, you will want AGM, or absorbed glass mat, batteries, which absorb gases (a result of battery charging) back into the battery rather than venting them outside the battery. AGM batteries are safe to keep inside your bus, and they won't spill acid if they tip over!

The two types of deep-cycle batteries most commonly used in off-grid skoolie systems are 6-volt and 12-volt. You can use either type to power a 12-volt electrical system, but if you're using 6-volt batteries, you need two batteries to get the same output as a single 12-volt battery.

Battery capacity is rated in amp-hours, or the number of amps (electrical current) that can flow from the battery in one hour. It is a common misconception that two 225-amp-hour 6-volt batteries will equal a 450-amp system, which is true only if you're using them in a 6-volt system. In a 12-volt system, those 225-amp-hour 6-volt batteries have the same output as one 225-amp-hour 12-volt battery.

That said, there are several reasons folks opt for 6-volt batteries, including a slightly lower total cost and the presumption that 6-volt batteries have fewer internal parts that can fail. On the other hand, going with 12-volt batteries saves you space (because you need only half as many batteries), which is a top priority in most skoolies! Also, the cost of extra cabling and terminals needed to connect 6-volt batteries quickly adds up, and it might not be worth the extra time and effort.

To determine how many batteries you need, use your total daily watt-hour estimate and roughly match that with the total battery capacity. However, it's not a one-to-one match but rather a one-to-two match. Here's why: For deep-cycle batteries to reach their peak lifespan, you shouldn't let them discharge below 50 percent of their total capacity before you recharge them (it has to do with battery chemistry). Effectively, this means that a 200-amp-hour battery should be used to supply only about 100 amp-hours of power before the battery gets recharged. The upshot? You need twice as many batteries.

At the beginning of the chapter, we used 1,500 watt-hours as a total figure for daily use, so we'll go with that to determine how many batteries we will need. Since battery capacity is rated in amp-hours, you can calculate how many watt-hours that equals by multiplying the amp-hours by the voltage rating. For example, a 250-amp-hour 12-volt battery will provide 3,000 watt-hours of power. Reducing that by 50 percent (due to the discharge issue), that battery is good for about 1,500 watt-hours — just enough to cover our daily usage of 1,500 watt-hours. However, it's better to install a slightly larger setup to provide for days when there is less sunshine to recharge the batteries with your solar panels. In this case, it might be wise to go with two 150-amp-hour or larger batteries.

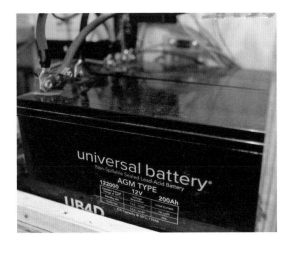

Battery SAFETY

Your skoolie layout plan must factor into the location of your batteries, and it's important to make sure the batteries are installed safely. Exposed terminal posts on batteries are extremely dangerous with any level of charge in the battery. Never make a connection between the positive and negative battery terminals. Even a brief accidental connection of the two battery terminals with a conductive material (like metal) can melt whatever is making the connection or start a fire. (If you're holding a wrench that touches both terminals, the wrench can actually melt in your hand!) Take your time installing the batteries and wiring, and always use insulated tools (no bare metal handles) when working with batteries.

Those same terminals are equally dangerous when the batteries are safely secured in your bus and wired to your solar system. Therefore, the battery space must include a cover that prevents accidental contact with the batteries, especially the battery terminals and wiring. If there are children in the bus, the cover MUST have a lock on it.

While sealed AGM batteries do not spill battery acid if they tip over — a primary reason I recommend them for your skoolie — they still pose a major safety hazard if they are not secured properly for traveling. I prefer to keep my batteries with my other utilities, primarily near the solar charge controller and power inverter. You can also locate the batteries in an underbody storage box or just under the foot of a bed. While AGM batteries are advertised as not needing ventilation, you should allow for a small space around or over the top of the batteries to ensure they have breathing room.

Follow all manufacturer's recommendations for wiring, storing, and ventilating batteries. Battery charging produces explosive gas. Sealed AGM batteries are designed to trap this gas inside the battery case, but it's possible that some gas may leak out. If this gas collects in an unventilated enclosed area, a nearby spark or flame could lead to an explosion.

MY FIRST SKOOLIE
THE AIRBNB BUS

THE FIRST SKOOLIE I CONVERTED, before I met Sabrina, was my 1997 International mid-size bus. I started renting it out on Airbnb, and it became a big hit before I had a chance to make any trips in it. I outfitted it really simply, with a full-size bed, a comfy futon, and a dining booth made from two of the bus seats. There's also a regular ice chest, a woodstove, and an air conditioner. For electricity, I have an extension cord running from the house to the bus.

MY FIRST SKOOLIE

AIRBNB BUS

Guests who stay there share the bathroom and kitchen in our house. We like to think of the Airbnb bus as a filter for people who aren't cool; we've had hundreds of exciting travelers from all around the world stay there. In a way, it feels as if we're on vacation with them!

12

CLIMATE *control*

When you picture yourself enjoying life in your skoolie, you probably envision sunshine and blue skies, but as we all know, freezing cold and extremely hot days are far too common! Fortunately, there are great options for keeping your bus-abode at a comfortable temperature. In addition to heating and cooling, you'll want some ventilation to keep your indoor air fresh and relatively dry.

COOLING *your skoolie*

KEEPING YOUR SKOOLIE cool can be done with fans or an air conditioner. There are many 12-volt fans on the market, but sometimes a fan isn't enough to contend with heat. An air conditioner is a real luxury for a skoolie, and it comes at a cost. Standard RV air conditioners mount to the roof and vent heat above the bus, which is very efficient compared to a portable air conditioner that puts off heat inside. The downside of an RV air-conditioner unit is that they can be expensive.

WINDOW/PORTABLE UNIT. A cheaper alternative is a window-style unit. A small- to medium-size window air conditioner that fits into a house window can work in your skoolie if you remove one of the windows and slide the back of the unit through the opening, then frame in the unit with wood to keep it in place.

The back of the air conditioner shouldn't protrude from the bus more than the side-view mirrors, so be sure to measure not only the unit's height and width (for window fitting) but also its depth (for fitting within the total width of the bus, including the mirrors). A variation of the window unit is the portable air conditioner, which connects to the window via a short duct. These can be easier to wrangle, and they simply roll into storage when they're not in use.

MINI-SPLIT. Another option is a ductless mini-split air-conditioning system. Mini-splits consist of a separate condenser and an indoor air handler and can provide both cooling and heating. The air handler is where the conditioned air blows, and it can be mounted inside the bus, along the back wall or above the side windows. The condenser can be mounted on a small platform or deck off the back of the

bus. Some skoolies have condensers mounted on their roof decks — just be cautious of your clearance (tractor trailers are limited to 13 feet 6 inches in height).

ROOF-MOUNTED RV UNIT. RV air-conditioner units are mounted on the roof, and a cutout is made in the roof for the air ducts to connect with the ceiling assembly, also known as the air distribution box (which is typically sold separately). Because cold air drops, this is an ideal mounting position for distributing the conditioned air. Any condensation that occurs will typically drain into a pan that is included with the unit, where it will evaporate. Most condensation pans have weep channels to allow excess condensation to simply drain onto the roof. A school bus's metal roof provides a great advantage over the materials used on RV roofs, which require routine maintenance and are prone to leaking and water damage over time.

Both mini-split systems and window air-conditioner systems require a household-style outlet, so you will have to either run them off of a generator or through a power inverter. RV rooftop air-conditioning units use household 115- or 120-volt power as well.

Note: Air conditioners create a spike in electrical current when they cycle on, known as the starting watts. While some systems have a soft-start feature that creates less of a spike, most do not, and your generator or power inverter needs to be rated for the starting watts.

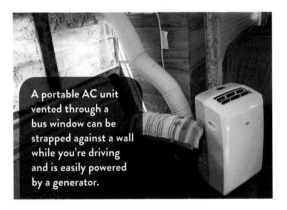

A portable AC unit vented through a bus window can be strapped against a wall while you're driving and is easily powered by a generator.

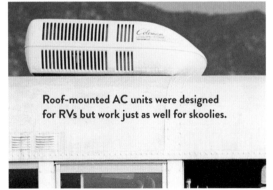

Roof-mounted AC units were designed for RVs but work just as well for skoolies.

Sizing an Air Conditioner

Before you decide on a method of cooling for your skoolie, first take into consideration how much space you have to cool and how much power the unit will require. Air conditioners are rated in British thermal units, or Btu. Typically, the smallest rating available is 5,000 Btu. One simple way to get a size estimate is to use an online Btu calculator and enter the internal dimensions of your bus as well as the insulation rating.

While most 12-volt fans can be powered with a solar system without too much energy strain, an air conditioner is a totally different animal. The amount of money you would have to spend to fully power your air conditioner with solar panels is significant, so a dedicated generator is most likely your easiest, most affordable option. It's nice to have a generator for backup energy in general, and if you have only a few weeks of extreme heat to deal with, it's probably not worth the investment for a massive solar system compared to a small generator. Be sure to note both the rated *startup* and running wattages of your air conditioner so that you can size the generator accordingly. Also, keep in mind that you can run your air conditioner off a large power inverter connected to the bus battery or alternator when driving.

A mini-split AC system has two parts: the inside box (above the windshield) that the air comes out of and an outside condenser box. Most mini-splits can both heat and cool.

HEATING *Your Skoolie*

HEATING YOUR SKOOLIE can be done with a woodstove, a liquid propane (LP) heater, or even a mini-split system, if you decided to go that route. Woodstoves in skoolies are extremely popular. There's nothing quite like cozying up to a woodstove in your home on a cold and dreary day, and the low cost of operation is the cherry on top!

Woodstoves

Before you jump to the classifieds to search for a woodstove, let's talk about why you don't want one too big or too small. First, if your bus is under 200 square feet inside, you do not want a small woodstove made for a house because it is likely rated for 400 square feet or more. You might be thinking, "Can't I just have a smaller

This tiny Dickinson wood stove mounts directly to a wall and takes up a minimal amount of space. Keep a saw handy to cut larger logs into small chunks to burn.

fire inside a larger stove?" Yes, you can build a smaller fire, but you won't get optimum performance from the stove this way, and you'll struggle to keep a smaller fire going. On the other hand, a woodstove that's too small will need firewood added frequently to keep it performing to its full potential, which still may not be enough to keep your bus warm and cozy!

While proper installation of your woodstove is extremely important for safety, choosing a woodstove that is EPA certified is crucial. Many old, noncertified woodstoves are still sought after, but the safety improvements that come with certified woodstoves make them a better choice for skoolies. EPA-certified woodstoves have improved airflow and better insulation to reduce smoke, resulting in a cleaner-burning, more efficient fire.

Thankfully, the popularity of tiny homes has created a market for small woodstoves, and that's great news for us skoolie people! Woodstoves for marine applications have also become popular for skoolies because they're designed for boat cabins that may be similar in size to an average bus interior.

Like air conditioners, woodstove sizes (or heat output) are rated in Btu. For example, the brand Cubic Mini offers a Cub model and a Grizzly model. The Grizzly is rated for 8,000 to 18,000 Btu and is suitable for heating 200 to

400 square feet, which would work for a mid- or full-size bus. For a short bus, you could opt for the Cub, which is designed for heating 100 to 200 square feet.

Most woodstoves are installed on the floor. Alternatively, there are stoves that can be wall mounted, such as Dickinson Marine's Newport Solid Fuel Heater. Cubic Mini also offers wall-mounted stoves. A wall-mounted stove saves on floor space and can be mounted on any wall surface inside the bus, including new walls that you build.

INSTALLING A WOODSTOVE

Installing your skoolie's woodstove correctly is crucial. The last thing you want is a fire-related disaster or a carbon monoxide leak! (See Everyone: Get a CO Detector! on page 171.)

PLACE THE STOVE. The first order of business is deciding where to place your woodstove and providing protection from its heat. It is essential to keep flammable items at a proper distance from the woodstove, and this includes walls. Most woodstoves require at least 3 feet of clearance from walls that lack a noncombustible barrier — too great a distance for a skoolie unless the stove is in the dead center of the bus. The solution is to install heat shields that go between the woodstove and nearby walls, cabinets, fixed-position furniture, and other combustibles.

INSTALL A HEAT SHIELD. To create a heat shield, begin by attaching a piece of fire-resistant drywall or mineral board directly to the bus walls or vulnerable furniture. Next, add a thin section of sheet metal over the fire-resistant board, but space it off by 1 inch to create an air space. You can use 1-inch sections of ⅜-inch copper pipe (or use large nuts) to space the sheet metal off the fire-resistant board. Then, screw through the sheet metal right through the inside of the spacer and into the wall to hold the shield in place. If your walls are drywall, you will have to go through the drywall and into the metal wall supports for a solid connection. As an added precaution, add a small heat shield between the stove's chimney pipe and window it runs in front to prevent heat fractures in the glass. A cool tip for reflecting heat around the stove piping is to use old license plates connected to each other!

The floor underneath and in front of the woodstove should be covered with nonflammable material, such as sheet metal.

A 4-inch hole saw is ideal for the 3-inch stove pipe most small wood stoves use. Having a little extra space around the pipe helps align it onto the stove.

PROVIDE A FLAME-RESISTANT HEARTH. To protect the floor from sparks and small coals that might exit the stove when you add firewood, mount your woodstove on a fire-resistant hearth made of ceramic tile, concrete pavers, natural stone, or even an old metal sign. A flame-retardant hearth rug is also a good option.

Even if you follow these basic installation recommendations, I suggest you also read over the International Building Code (IBC) specifications for woodstove installations to better understand the safety concerns and potential regulations.

DETERMINE PLACEMENT OF THE CHIMNEY PIPE. Next comes the most challenging and intimidating part of a woodstove installation: the dreaded roof hole for the chimney pipe. Cutting a big hole in your roof is a scary thought, but it must be done. Some folks run their chimney pipe through the side of their bus by removing a window and framing in around the chimney pipe with sheet metal, but bends in a chimney can reduce the drafting of smoke and lead to buildup of hazardous creosote (soot). If you decide to go through the side rather than the roof, be prepared for a more complicated chimney pipe route, more frequent cleaning, and potentially less-efficient fires.

CALCULATE THE SIZE OF THE ROOF HOLE. Calculating the proper size of roof hole can be tricky. For instance, Cubic Mini stoves use a 3-inch chimney pipe, so one would think the roof hole would be 3 inches as well . . . not so! That 3-inch measurement is for the internal diameter of the pipe; your roof hole must allow for a wider external diameter. An extra ½ to 1 inch of perimeter clearance around the stovepipe (totaling an additional 1 to 2 inches in diameter larger than the exterior of the stovepipe) is ideal when passing through the roof. This means a 3-inch stovepipe needs a 4- or 5-inch-diameter roof opening.

LOCATE AND MARK THE ROOF HOLE. The best way to cut the roof hole is with a hole saw, which you can find anywhere power tools are sold. A hole saw attaches to a power drill and has a center drill bit (for creating a starter hole and anchoring the saw) and a large cylinder with saw teeth for cutting the full hole. Before locating the stovepipe hole, secure the woodstove in its desired position.

Remember: Be sure to position the stove so that the chimney pipe doesn't hit any of the roof supports, as these cannot be cut.) Some stoves, like the Cubic Minis, come with predrilled screw holes on the inside of their legs for attaching the stove to the hearth. Other stoves require some kind of custom attachment setup. One option is to attach L brackets to the stove's legs with self-tapping screws, and then screw the other leg of the bracket to the floor (through the hearth and into the subfloor).

To mark the location of the stovepipe hole in the roof, make sure the bus is on level ground,

so the bus floor is level. Tie a bolt or nut onto a string and hold the string against the ceiling, with the bolt or nut hanging down slightly higher than the stove (you're creating a make-shift plumb bob; if you own a plumb bob, use that instead). Position the string so the weighted end is centered over the stovepipe outlet (let the string stop swinging so it's hanging straight down). Mark the string's position on the ceiling. Drill a small hole through the ceiling at the marked line, using a standard drill bit. This hole will act as a pilot hole for your hole saw location on the roof; it must be smaller in diameter than the center bit of the hole saw.

Be aware that there are two layers of metal to pass through, unless you've taken apart the ceiling and have not yet installed the new ceiling. As always, wear protection when drilling and have an assistant steady the bottom of your ladder while you work!

CUT FROM THE ROOF DOWN. Make the chimney hole from the top side of the roof. Center the hole saw bit into the pilot hole you drilled from inside and start out slowly. The hole saw will slowly and steadily cut away the metal circle. When it is almost through, the hole saw may get caught on edges that aren't fully cut yet and spin the drill, so use caution, and keep two hands on the drill at all times.

After you're through the first layer, the ceiling layer is next. Expect some debris to fall into the bus, so put down a protective cloth

or have someone hold a bucket or trash can up against the ceiling, under the hole saw's exit point. Any insulation that comes from the hole can be thrown away. (It's okay if insulation touches the stovepipe because it poses no fire hazard.) When the deed is done, you will have a sharp round circle that used to be part of your skoolie roof as a souvenir. Take a picture of that big hole in your roof and share it with all your buddies, who will likely think you're nuts!

NEW-STOVE *Smell*

Be sure to keep the bus well ventilated during the first few burns in a new stove because the factory paint will put off a strong odor. The paint is not fully cured until the stove is used a few times. If possible, it's even better to have a few fires in the stove before you install it in the bus.

Flexible silicone flashing boots are great because they thoroughly seal around the pipe, even on the curved bus roof. Add caulking between the flashing and roof before attaching it with self-tapping screws; also add some high-temperature caulk where the pipe itself meets the flashing.

Slip the chimney rain cap over the top of the pipe, and use a few self-tapping screws to secure it in place.

CONNECT THE REMAINING PIPE AND INSTALL THE FLASHING. Now, connect the remaining sections of stovepipe (they usually come in 24- to 36-inch sections), and install the chimney flashing. Chimney flashing is the part that surrounds the pipe and seals the space between the pipe and the roof. Regular house roofs use metal flashing, but school buses have curved roofs that make using traditional flashing challenging. Fortunately, there's a great solution: high-temperature silicone pipe flashing. Silicone flashing is flexible and can be trimmed with scissors or a utility knife to fit your pipe, and it conforms to the curve of your roof.

The numbers on the flashing represent different pipe diameters, and you use these as a guide when trimming the top of the silicone collar to fit your pipe. If you bought flashing that fits a 2-inch to 6-inch pipe, and your stove uses a 3-inch pipe, you will cut the silicone lip of the flashing at the 3-inch mark. Then, you simply slide the flashing over the pipe and down to the roof. For added insurance, put exterior-grade silicone caulk between the flashing and the roof, and seal the pipe to the flashing with high-temperature caulk. Use short self-tapping screws to hold the flashing flush with the roof, driving a screw every inch around the perimeter. The flashing includes a metal layer for screwing through.

ADD A RAIN CAP. With your woodstove, chimney pipe, and flashing installed, you can now add a chimney rain cap that will prevent rainwater from getting inside. Secure the rain cap with a couple self-tapping screws, going through the cap and into the pipe. Rain caps that include wire mesh will help keep unwanted things from getting inside the pipe (such as birds) as well as flying out (such as sparks).

Propane Heaters

A liquid propane (LP) heater for your skoolie is another heating option, and one that poses negatives and positives. Mr. Heater makes a portable, indoor-safe propane heater designed for small spaces, but when it's set on high, it burns through a small canister of propane in just a few hours — although there is a kit available to connect the Mr. Heater to a larger propane tank, such as the type used for propane barbecue grills. You can also find many indoor, wall-mounted propane heaters for sale.

Many folks are nervous about dealing with propane gas. That's understandable. But if you feel confident about using propane for heat, you can select from tanks that can be hard-mounted on the exterior of your bus, such as tank carriers that most travel trailers use, and tanks that install horizontally under the bus. The latter hold more propane than a barbecue grill–size tank, but they are more costly, and not all propane suppliers can fill this style of tank.

My favorite propane hack is to use the standard 20-gallon barbecue grill–style propane tanks that you can simply swap out at a grocery store, hardware store, or home center, making it easy to refill while on the road. You can mount the tank on the back of your bus with an RV propane carrier.

I suggest keeping a Mr. Heater handy for emergency use when wood is not available. But for the majority of winter-temperature control, I far prefer the simplicity of a woodstove. An added bonus of a woodstove is its ability to dry out your bus. The less moisture you have inside your skoolie, the better!

"Mr. Heater" makes several small, indoor-safe propane heaters that use one-pound propane canisters. They can also be connected to a larger propane tank with an extension hose.

Everyone: GET A CO DETECTOR!

A carbon monoxide (CO) detector is an absolute MUST in your bus. This device will warn you of problems not only with a woodstove, a propane heater, or other combustion appliance but also with the bus's exhaust system — in case of an exhaust leak underneath the bus. Carbon monoxide is an odorless, colorless, *and deadly* gas. Many CO-poisoning deaths happen while the victims are asleep.

Carbon monoxide detectors can be found at any hardware store or home improvement center. Be sure to get the battery-powered versions instead of those designed to be hardwired to a home system with a battery just for backup.

Install a detector in your skoolie *now* — it's *always* better to be safe than sorry.

CO detector

VENTING *Your Skoolie*

EXHAUST FANS, or vent fans, help remove moisture from your bus. If you've ever slept in a van, you will recall the fogged windows in the morning. This is moisture you have created that has nowhere to escape. Moisture will collect on windows especially and can drip down along the walls and eventually lead to mold or rust.

A vent fan can be a small fan that fits in a window or, better yet, a roof fan (such as a Fan-Tastic) fitted into the roof hatch opening or installed in a newly cut hole in the bus roof. Many small fans are sold in 12-volt versions. Roof fans require a cutout in your ceiling to accept the fan's housing, which fits over the top of the cutout. A lip surrounds the fan housing and is slightly wider than the perimeter of the cutout. Self-tapping screws and caulking hold the assembly in place and seal the opening from rain.

Vent fans can be problematic and even dangerous if you don't use them properly. Ventilation isn't just about moisture; it's also about air circulation or, more precisely, air exchange. A fan sucks air out of a living space. This means that you need to let fresh air into the space to replace the removed air. This fresh air is called makeup air and is critical to healthy and safe ventilation. You can provide for makeup air simply by cracking a window or door or installing a screened intake vent that you close when it's not in use.

If you run a vent fan without providing means for makeup air, the fan will try to pull in air through cracks along window frames and other tiny breaches in the bus envelope. This may work fine when the woodstove isn't running. However, if you have a fire going in the stove, a lack of makeup air can result in the vent fan pulling toxic fumes and smoke into the room rather than letting it go up the chimney (an effect called backdrafting). Even if you're cooking with propane, which doesn't require a chimney, it's a good idea to provide makeup air if the vent fan is running.

Makeup air at any time will help your fan do its job faster and more effectively, and it will make the ambient air in the bus fresher.

A roof vent fan will help move moist air out of your skoolie and maintain a steady flow of fresh air.

The FAIR-WEATHER BUS

The ultimate low-budget (and most fun) way to keep your skoolie climate controlled is to simply follow the weather! If you're building a skoolie for travel, why not save on the extra complications of heating and cooling and just be nomadic?

TYLER AND LEXI
ONE WILD RIDE BUS
@ONEWILDRIDEBUS

TYLER AND LEXI found the 10-window, DT466E-powered 2001 International bus of their dreams in an online ad. They started converting it in August of 2017 and were ready to hit the road by spring of 2018. Now they live in the bus full time and have traveled to 19 states so far.

Their main goal with the conversion was to make sure the bus felt homey and warm — not like a traditional motor home. And when they were searching for a bus, they knew they wanted one with a handicapped entrance at the back, so that they could open the door when they were in bed! The bus has lots of comfy seating areas, too: a custom sofa along the passenger-side wall and a dining booth behind the driver's seat.

ONE WILD RIDE BUS

@onewildridebus

ONE WILD RIDE
EST. 2017

Along with the comfortable feel, the bus is also very practical. There are kitchen cabinets on both sides of the bus, a 54-gallon water container that's stored under the bed, a composting toilet, an indoor shower, and even a "garage" area for storing a generator, tools, and various gear.

Lexi and Tyler say, "The best part of skoolie life so far has been the community! One thing we've learned along the way is not to be scared to ask for advice. We've gotten some of our best ideas that way and have found the best boondocking spots from fellow skoolie friends."

13

WATER and PLUMBING

How exciting is the idea of having running water in your school bus dwelling?! Being able to turn a faucet on and off for water is a true luxury when living off-grid, but it's entirely feasible thanks to efficient water pumps and food-grade tanks. In this chapter I'll touch on options for water supply and drainage, from simple to complex and from cheap to costly.

WATER USAGE, STORAGE, *and* SUPPLY

BEFORE WE BEGIN detailing different water system setups, first let's take into consideration how much water you plan to use and how complex a system you are willing to invest in and construct. According to the United States Geological Survey, the average person uses 80 to 100 gallons of water per day. Obviously, you will have to make some extreme changes to your skoolie lifestyle if you fit this definition of an average user!

Practice water-saving techniques at home to see how comfortable you are with reduction efforts, such as turning the shower off while you shampoo and soap up, then back on for a final rinse. You can greatly minimize water use while brushing your teeth and doing dishes as well. Just don't cut back on the water intake you need to keep your body hydrated!

Water storage is your starting point for any system, large or small. For health and safety's sake, choose a storage tank that meets U.S. Food and Drug Administration guidelines for food-grade containers. Containers range from 7 gallons (usually available at a big box store) to 46 gallons (which you can find online).

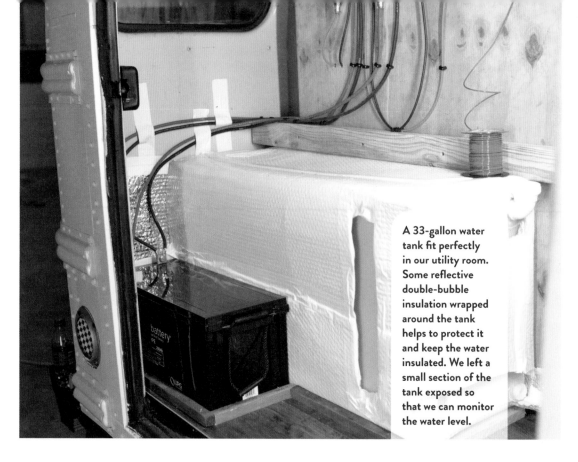

A 33-gallon water tank fit perfectly in our utility room. Some reflective double-bubble insulation wrapped around the tank helps to protect it and keep the water insulated. We left a small section of the tank exposed so that we can monitor the water level.

Mounting your water container inside is much easier than mounting it under your bus, and an inside container is away from road debris that could puncture the tank. If you do decide to mount a tank on the underside of your skoolie, use 1½-inch slotted angle metal and grade 8 bolts (rated for automotive use) to make a cradle-style frame. Attach the cradle to the bus body frame rails that run perpendicular to the main chassis frame rails. Blackwater and graywater tanks can be hung under the bus in the same manner (we'll discuss those on page 184).

Gravity-Fed Supply

A simple gravity-fed system is the cheapest option for providing running water in your bus. You can install a water tank above your sink or showerhead or on a dedicated shelf with heavy-duty brackets and add a valve to the tank to turn the water flow on and off. The great thing about gravity-fed systems — aside from their low cost — is the ease of installing and maintaining them. There are no hidden water lines that are vulnerable to leaks that can damage your bus, and in the winter you can remove the tank to prevent it from freezing when you aren't using the bus. Also, you can easily take the tank out of the bus to use it elsewhere.

Filling a gravity-fed system is often just a matter lifting out the tank and filling it at a sink or outdoor spigot. A popular technique is to keep multiple small water tanks on hand to swap out as needed when a fill-up location isn't available. If you permanently attach the tank, however, you will need to fill it with a drinking-water-safe hose.

The primary negative of a gravity-fed system is the small tank size, necessitating frequent fill-ups. Also, you need a dedicated tank for each faucet. An elaborate gravity-fed system could be split to multiple faucets, but in this case you might as well install a water pump because the time and effort will be similar.

Pumping Water

Water tank and pump setups are not as complicated to design as you might think, thanks to the market created by RV manufacturers. Once you've decided on a tank size and location, you can pick up a 12-volt pump and a few system accessories compatible with the pump. Shurflo is the big name in 12-volt water supply pumps, but there are other manufacturers.

One key accessory is a pipe strainer, which mounts between the tank and pump to filter out debris. On online shopping sites, pipe strainers usually are listed right along with the pumps and water accumulator tanks. An accumulator tank mounts just after the pump, and its job is to accumulate pressurized water to reduce the number of times the pump kicks on and off, thus saving energy. When you're brushing your teeth, it's nice to not have the pump turning on and off with each rinse.

Speaking of energy: when factoring a water pump into your watt-hour figure, rest assured that the pump consumes power only when a faucet is on and the accumulator tank is empty. Most 12-volt water pumps are quite efficient when used conservatively.

A 7-gallon water container mounted over a salad bowl-turned sink is super easy to set up. The wastewater drains into another container under the sink that can be emptied at the same time you refill the water jug.

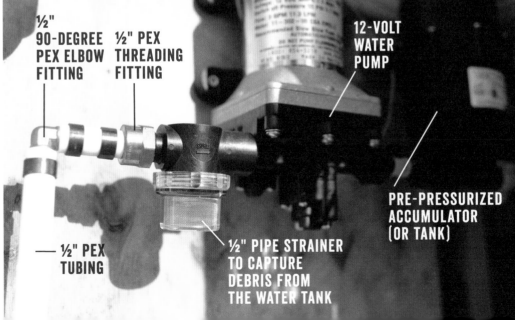

½"
90-DEGREE
PEX ELBOW
FITTING

½" PEX
THREADING
FITTING

12-VOLT
WATER
PUMP

½" PEX
TUBING

½" PIPE STRAINER
TO CAPTURE
DEBRIS FROM
THE WATER TANK

PRE-PRESSURIZED
ACCUMULATOR
(OR TANK)

Making PLUMBING CONNECTIONS

PLUMBING THE WATER supply to your kitchen or bathroom will require water lines and fittings to connect those lines. The keyword for this process is *PEX*. PEX is plastic (technically, cross-linked polyethylene) tubing that is flexible, resistant to freezing, and relatively simple to connect with push-in fittings or crimp rings. Crimp rings require a specific crimp tool sold at home centers and plumbing suppliers. You can use ½-inch PEX tubing for all water supply connections in a skoolie.

While PEX tubing is slightly flexible and can make gentle bends, you must use fittings to make sharp turns. Conventional PEX connections employ barbed fittings (that fit inside the tubing) and crimp rings (that fit over the tubing and clamp it to the fitting inside the tubing). Push-in fittings (the best-known brand is SharkBite) do not need crimp rings: the PEX tubing simply pushes into the fitting and can only be removed with a special removal tool. The tool is a small piece of plastic shaped like a horseshoe; it costs a few bucks. Push-in fittings are more expensive than barbed fittings and crimp rings, but the crimp tool is expensive, so push-in fittings might be best for your skoolie. SharkBite and other brands make all the fittings you will need, in addition to tube clamps that hold tubing safely out of the way in a desired location.

PEX CRIMPING TOOL

PEX FITTINGS

PEX CRIMP RINGS

PEX TUBING CUTTER

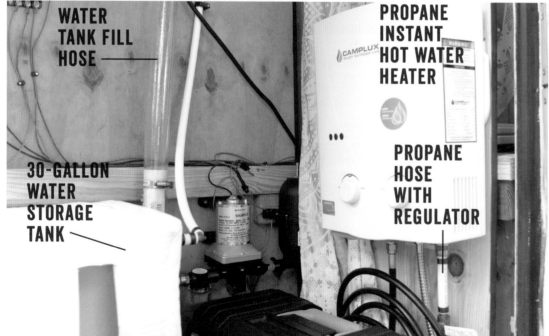

WATER TANK FILL HOSE

PROPANE INSTANT HOT WATER HEATER

30-GALLON WATER STORAGE TANK

PROPANE HOSE WITH REGULATOR

Cutting PEX tubing with a tubing cutter

The crimp ring is slipped onto the tubing, then the fitting is inserted into the tubing. The crimp ring is compressed with a crimping tool to secure the fitting.

A PEX "Go/No Go" tool verifies that the crimp is complete.

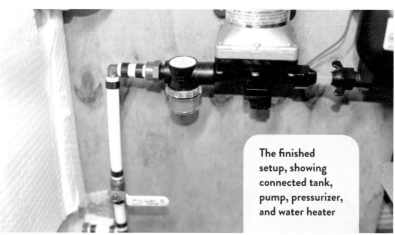

The finished setup, showing connected tank, pump, pressurizer, and water heater

The faucet you choose may have a larger fitting than the ½-inch PEX line, in which case you will need a faucet compression connector or conversion fitting to adapt the line to the faucet. If you plan to have only cold water available, you can use a "cold tap" style of faucet or you can use a standard faucet (with hot and cold taps) and install a cap on the inlet for the hot-water faucet valve.

Plumbing a drainpipe to a graywater tank under your bus can be done with standard PVC pipe going from the sink drain down to the graywater tank. PVC plumbing pipe and fittings are easy to assemble with PVC solvent glue. Some fittings, like connections for a P-trap, use basic threaded connections so you can remove the parts if necessary.

DEALING *with* WASTEWATER

ALL WATER THAT flows out from your sinks, tub, shower, and toilet is wastewater and must be dealt with in a safe and legal fashion. Wastewater from the bathroom sink and tub or shower is considered *graywater*. Wastewater from the toilet and kitchen sink (according to most local regulations) is *blackwater*. Graywater and blackwater have different disposal requirements and restrictions, with blackwater rules being much more stringent, understandably.

In most skoolies and other mobile off-grid homes, the toilet does not utilize water, which greatly simplifies blackwater drainage in the bathroom. As for the blackwater from the kitchen sink, you will need to collect this in an RV blackwater holding tank with 3-inch valves that can be emptied at an RV park, using a holding tank hose. If you commit to using only eco-friendly (nontoxic, biodegradable) soaps and filter out all food scraps and other nonliquid material going down the sink, you may be able to utilize a graywater tank instead, depending on local law.

Graywater can be disposed of at an RV park as well, and the required tank valve size is 1½ inches. If you have a full tank and nowhere to dump, you can drain the tank into a portable wastewater tote that can be easily rolled to and from a graywater dump station.

You can collect graywater in a tank that goes under the bathroom sink or mounts to the bus chassis under the floor. A short PVC pipe from the bottom of the sink drain to the graywater container works great, and any odors from the tank can be addressed with a small splash of bleach. You can also add a water P-trap to the sink drainpipe (if space allows) that will prevent the backflow of odors. All sink and tub/shower drains in regular houses have a P-trap. It's a U-shaped section of pipe that holds a small amount of water to seal the drain and prevent gases and odors from rising up from the sewer drain — or, in the case of a skoolie, up from a storage tank — out through the sink drain opening.

Always use environmentally friendly soaps that make it safe for you to dump the wastewater. Also, your graywater tank doesn't need to be FDA approved as food-grade.

The custom graywater tank for this bus is made with two 8-foot lengths of 4-inch PVC pipe joined with elbows at one end. The other end includes reducers, a P-trap, and a 1½-inch faucet valve for draining the tank.

HOT WATER

HOT WATER IS a true luxury for skoolies! If you plan to live full time or make frequent long trips in your skoolie, why not have hot water available for a hot shower every now and then? After a long day of hiking through any one of the gorgeous parks in the United States, a shower in the evening is truly the icing on the cake.

Go Tankless

A point-of-use, or tankless, water heater is the best option for your skoolie unless you're willing to power a small hot-water tank that uses a fair amount of electricity (because it keeps the water hot at all times) and takes up added space.

Small tankless water heaters can be electric or propane. Electric units require a sizable amount of energy, usually at 240 volts, so be prepared to run one with a gas generator. There are 110/120-volt versions, but they will still use up to 30 amps. If you are conservative with your shower times, you won't have to run the generator for very long.

PROPANE WORKS BEST FOR MOST. Propane tankless water heaters are an excellent choice because they require a minimal amount of energy and allow you to have plenty of hot water at the ready. There are also propane water heaters that require only a couple batteries to ignite the propane flame that generates the hot water, as opposed to having to connect it to a 12-volt power source.

A water heater requires pressurized water, and your 12-volt water pump will share the duty of pumping water to your cold sink tap and to the water heater. For the basic installation, you need a PEX T-fitting (conventional or push-in) that installs after the water pump, followed by a section of PEX tubing between one of the outlets of the T-fitting and the cold-water input on the heater. You then connect another section of PEX tubing to the hot-water output on the heater and run this to your hot-water fixture, whether it's a showerhead or sink faucet.

Most tankless water heaters have adjustment knobs to dial in the temperature you want without having to adjust a separate cold-water valve. Eccotemp makes a tankless propane water heater with a digital temperature control that is fully adjustable.

ADD SHUTOFF VALVES. If your bus will be subject to freezing temperatures (most will), it's a good idea to add shutoff valves in-line between the heater and the pump and between the heater and the faucet. These allow you to isolate the heater from the water supply and drain the heater to prevent water from freezing inside the water heater on cold days.

Most water heaters have drains to get the excess water out of the heater.

For a propane-type water heater, you also need a propane tank connected to the heater via a propane hose. I suggest mounting the propane tank to the back of the bus and keeping the water heater somewhere toward the back interior with ample clearance for ease of access.

There are a variety of propane tanks available, including horizontal tanks that can mount permanently under the bus, but these are quite expensive. I have found that standard 20-gallon grill-style propane tanks work well and are easy to swap out and get refilled. Of course, each water heater will have specific installation guidelines that may vary from model to model, but most function the same way.

Solar Is Another Option

Other options for hot water include solar showers or bladders that use the sun to warm the water. There are also lots of DIY options for building your own solar water heater using CPVC pipes painted black and fittings for attaching a water hose. In addition, there are all-in-one camp shower units, such as the Coleman H2Oasis, that include a propane water heater and a built-in water pump.

A simple solution for showering is the solar bag shower; just fill it, let it warm up in the sunshine, and shower away!

This custom propane carrier is designed for two standard grill-size propane tanks; these are easily filled or exchanged while on the road.

TROY AND CINDY

WHITE WHALE SKOOLIE

@WHITEWHALESKOOLIE

AFTER LEAVING THEIR JOBS, selling their large home, and spending weeks hunting for just the right bus, Troy and Cindy found a full-size 2003 International to convert. Originally, it seated 72 passengers; now they live in it year round. In the summer, they park the bus (which they call the White Whale) and work on a farm. In the winter, they travel. So far, they've driven their bus more than 13,000 miles around the United States.

Inside the White Whale is a mix of custom-made and repurposed items. Troy and Cindy added custom cabinets in the kitchen, but they reused the foam from the original bus seats to make couch cushions.

There's a vintage woodstove along with a new Dickinson propane heater (see page 171), to keep things warm in the wintertime. There's also a large livestock tank that serves as a bathtub.

Troy and Cindy have made use of every possible space on the bus — including the roof, where there are six 100-watt solar panels connected to an MPPT solar controller that keeps their three 155-amp-hour AGM batteries charged. In addition to the solar panels, there's also a small roof platform with wood decking and a welded metal frame.

14 DETAILING *Your* SKOOLIE

Never underestimate the potential for additional details and customization during home construction, even if the home is less than 200 square feet! There are endless possibilities for making your skoolie unique and personal. There are also a few practical matters to address, like privacy, security, and, of course, home storage. This chapter has tips and inspiration to get you started. I'm sure you'll have no problem taking it from here!

Decorative window film is easy to trim and install on windows to provide privacy without compromising extra light.

Magnetic hooks are a must for your skoolie! They work great for a number of tasks, including holding curtains in place.

PRIVACY *and* SECURITY

IN A HOME with windows running the entire length of the dwelling, privacy is certainly a challenge. For many folks, curtains are a must, and there many ways to install them. Basic rod-and-hanger kits can be mounted over windows. Purchased half-window curtains (café curtains) nicely cover bus windows without excess fabric hanging below the windows. Thermal curtains are excellent because they help insulate the skoolie interior from cold, drafty windows (again, the leading source of temperature flow in a bus). Also, why not see if a family member, friend, or local business is willing to make custom curtains for you with whatever material you desire?

Another way to add privacy is with window-cling privacy films. These come in many decorative styles and are relatively easy to install on your skoolie windows. Installing film works the same way as window tint: clean the window thoroughly, mist the glass with water, then peel and stick the film onto the window while using a flat squeegeelike tool to smooth out bubbles. (See Tinting or Covering Bus windows on page 107 for more information on window tints.)

Thanks to the wealth of metal in your bus, you can also use magnets to hang tapestries or sheers for privacy or as interior decor. Magnet hooks are handy both inside and outside of skoolies for hanging up items or holding objects in place.

Next is security: How will you lock the doors on your skoolie? After all, securing your skoolie is just as important as securing your home. There are several approaches.

When you're inside the skoolie, the main front doorway can be locked from the inside with a deadbolt or a heavy-duty gate latch. A traditional deadbolt works with a swinging-type door and requires drilling a hole in the doorway large enough for the lock's bolt to fit into. Accordion-style entrance doors can be held shut using gate lock hardware or by installing a deadbolt lock inside the door in the same fashion as in a standard house door. Because the bus door is metal, this requires an appropriately sized hole saw or large drill bit designed for drilling metal.

When you leave your bus, you can lock the front door on the exterior side with a hasp latch secured with a padlock. Install the hasp with self-tapping screws or through bolts.

The rear emergency exit door can be secured by locking the interior handle in its sealed position. Rear door handles vary from bus to bus, but typically you can drill a hole through both the handle and a fixed point on the door to allow for a bolt or lock to fit through, preventing the handle from being opened. The door can also be locked from the inside with a gate latch or a deadbolt lock.

A large gate slide-bolt latch attached to the inside of the entrance door will prevent the door from being opened from the outside.

HAVE AN *Escape Plan*

In case of an emergency, be sure you have an escape plan. School buses have numerous emergency exits, but not everyone can easily hop out of a bus. Take the time to inspect the emergency exit windows, hatch, and rear door so that if an emergency happens, you are prepared. Emergency windows completely fold or swing out, opening up a 2 × 2-foot space for exiting. Roof hatches (if they weren't used for a vent fan) have similar openings. Make sure emergency exits are not locked from the outside (when the bus is occupied) and can be easily opened from the inside.

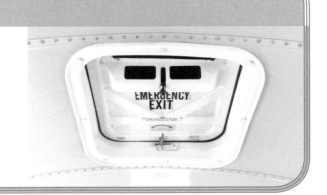

This massive drawer easily slides out from under the queen bed, thanks to felt pads installed on the bottom. A small latch holds it in place when the bus is in motion.

Underbody storage boxes range from 24 to 72 inches wide and can be bolted to the bus body frame rails.

STORAGE

STORAGE SPACE IS one of those things you can never have too much of! You will be amazed by how many essential items you'll need for just a weekend getaway. The area under your bed will likely be the largest potential storage area on your skoolie, even if part of that space is devoted to water or solar battery storage.

BUILT-IN UNDERBED DRAWERS. One of the best ways to utilize underbed storage space is with built-in drawers. Building drawers from scratch can be a time-consuming, challenging process, but you can easily find used chests of drawers to repurpose. You might use 2×3 lumber to construct your own frames for the individual drawers to fit into, or for a classy look, cut the face frame (the decorative front pieces) from a chest and mount pieces of it under the bed to hold the drawers. You will still need to construct some support for the rear of the drawer, though.

For storage elsewhere, shelves can be run almost anywhere along the sides the bus, and a large shelf can be installed up front, over the driver's area. Table booth seats, sofa bases, end tables, and many other pieces of furniture often can serve double duty as storage trunks. When you're living in a small space, it's important to design items to have dual purposes!

A rear deck provides ample space for propane tank and generator storage! We built ours out of steel pipe and flanges bolted to the back bumper, topped with pressure-treated lumber.

THE BACK DECK. You can add a back deck for storage and for mounting propane tanks or generators to the back of your skoolie. A short skoolie deck can serve not only as a surface for propane tanks and generators but also as storage space for outdoor items that can withstand weather. You can build a basic structure with galvanized steel plumbing pipe (the silver galvanized pipe; not the black steel pipe, which will rust). Start with four to six threaded steel pipe flanges bolted to the back bumper. Screw short sections of threaded pipe into the flanges to create supports for deck boards made of pressure-treated lumber. You can use ratchet straps to hold a generator and storage box in place, and you can mount an RV propane tank holder directly to the deck boards.

UNDERBODY STORAGE. Underbody storage boxes are great because they make use of what is otherwise unused: dead space beneath your bus. These boxes range from 24 to 72 inches wide, 16 to 20 inches deep,

and 16 to 24 inches tall. If you get a 36-inch underbody box, for example, you will cut out a 36½-inch-wide opening from the lower bus body (using your grinder), then fit the underbody box into the opening. To hold the box in place, welded frame brackets are available, but you can use slotted metal angle to affix the box to the bus body rails, similar to how you would install a graywater or blackwater tank.

The Battle of the Rattle

The Battle of the Rattle is something all skoolie owners deal with. With a full chorus of home supplies riding behind you, some racket is to be expected. And because diesel engines idle at very low rpm, vibrations when idling are nearly unavoidable. But there are ways to diminish the din!

Metal-on-metal rattles can be lessened by tightening any associated screws or bolts, and also by wedging something between the two pieces. Wood-to-metal contact can create

squeaks, in which case you will want to *decrease* the tightness of the contact. Woodstove rattles can be minimized with bungee cords holding things down, and miscellaneous kitchen rattles can be muted by placing towels between or under metal pieces. Even with these precautions, don't be surprised if after driving 1,000 miles with minimal noises, a new wicked rattle randomly begins! Sometimes the best solution is to crank up the stereo (see page 197).

Securing items in place is common sense, but you'd be surprised at how easily things can come loose in a bus. Door latches, hook-and-eye latches, and bungee cords will help hold loose objects in place for the most part, but heavier items may require ratchet straps, especially items toward the back of the bus, where movement is amplified behind the rear axle. Just keep plenty of ratchet straps (for heavy-duty hold-downs) and bungee cords (for lightweight items) on hand for traveling, and you'll be fine.

Whether you're people-watching at festivals or carrying kayaks, a roof deck is the ultimate exterior upgrade for a skoolie!

AMENITIES

AMENITIES INCLUDE ANYTHING you can add on to your skoolie to make it more functional or simply feel more like home.

STEREO SYSTEMS are a necessity, end of story. You can wire in a regular car stereo to your bus's 12-volt fuse block, or you can make use of a big Bluetooth speaker. I personally don't see why one would need more than one source for audio in a skoolie, so I support the Bluetooth speaker route 100 percent! You can tote it with you wherever you go, and it is a cinch to set up. For a full-on stereo system with numerous speakers, amps, and subs, you will have to incorporate the entire setup into your build to make space for speakers and wiring. If this is a priority for you, then by all means go for it!

AWNINGS are a key part of just about any RV, so why not have one for your skoolie? You can install an awning kit designed for RVs, or you can purchase a smaller awning designed for vans and SUV roof racks. ARB and Smittybilt are two manufacturers of awnings that market heavily to van-life folks, and their awnings are great for providing a nice shady area beside your bus. Both of these awning options will cost a pretty penny, but there is an alternative! You can call it a hack, or just common sense, but connecting a sun shade sail to the side of your bus works wonders.

To add a sun shade sail, buy some D-ring tie-downs and attach them above the windows with short self-tapping screws. Hook the sail to the D-rings, and prop up the outside corners with painter extension poles (the telescoping type), using rope and tent stakes to pull the shade tightly over the poles and down to the ground. This doesn't take any longer to set up than a traditional awning, it costs a quarter of the price, and it looks great! A quick tip: If you have the space to store a couple 6- to 7-foot bamboo poles, they make stylish and cheap substitutes for painter poles.

ROOF DECKS! I could write an entire chapter on building a roof deck, but I'll just leave you with some quick thoughts to tickle your fancy. Roof decks are awesome because they add real estate to your home, a fun place to chill with friends, and a great place to soak up all the great views you'll find while living the skoolie life. Also, roof decks offer a more private location for meditating, practicing yoga, or just relaxing.

To construct one style of a roof deck, start with vertical metal posts anchored to the outside of the bus wall supports that run between the windows. Next, attach wood or metal joists between the posts, parallel with the side walls, above the highest point of the bus. Once the sides of the roof deck are trimmed and bolted

Personalizing your skoolie is what will make it truly feel like home.

in place, you can trust it will last you for years to come. Other deck designs include boards spanning across the roof, bolted down with custom brackets, or boards running lengthwise (front to back) that act as joists for deck boards. Some folks have even used their old bus seat frames to create a level surface along the sides of their bus that decking can attach to. At any rate, there are no standard ways for building a skoolie roof deck, but for safety's sake, don't take shortcuts.

BACKUP CAMERAS improve safety and give you peace of mind when maneuvering your bus. A kit designed for recreational vehicles will fit your skoolie, and you can power it off your engine's 12-volt power system.

BIKE RACKS for skoolies are simple to install. Get a heavy-duty fork-mount holder for each bike. Use self-tapping screws to secure the fork mounts to the back of the bus. Mount a cargo hook below to connect a bungee cord for holding the rear wheel in place. Be sure to have a second set of hands holding the bike in place while you tighten the fork mount. You can store the front wheel inside the bus or attach it to the rear wheel with additional bungee cords.

FINISHING TOUCHES for your skoolie are entirely up to you! The whole idea is to make your bus feel like home, so objects that mean a lot to you — whether they include favorite artwork, fun-loving fabrics, or a family memento or heirloom — should find a place in your skoolie.

Time to hit the road!

ACKNOWLEDGMENTS

TO MY BEST FRIEND, Sabrina Hartley, I owe many thanks for endless support throughout the publication of this book — from motivating me to work steadily on the manuscript to working the saws while I shouted measurements. I couldn't have done this without your love and care.

Special thanks to Zachary Roberts for lending his expertise on short notice to turn a dresser into a kitchen counter, complete with sink and plumbing accommodations.

Thank you, Kevin Rudisill for helping with interior framing and the woodstove installation, and for being great company.

Thank you, Carleen Madigan, the editor who went above and beyond to make this book come together.

Thank you, Eli Meir Kaplan for being an outstanding photographer and great company throughout the construction process.

Thanks to my father, Donald Sutherland, for not hesitating to drive 12 hours to help bring the Book Bus home to West Virginia.

Many thanks to the wonderful folks who helped with odds and ends, painting, and participating in the photo shoots: Cori Berlin, Kimberly Hyatt, Oz Ewell, Elsa Plott, Dylan Sutherland, Luke Collins, Mike Eshleman, Dana Anders, Lillian Potter-Saum, and our neighbors Grady and Jocee Baracka.

OUR BUS'S BUDGET

BUS ACQUISITION COSTS

1996 International mid-size bus	$4,000
Starting batteries (2)	$225
Inspection	$250
Total	**$4,475**

POWER SUPPLY

2000-watt portable inverter generator	$455
Weatherproof generator cover	$15
12-volt 200-AH AGM deep-cycle battery	$348
100-watt 12-volt monocrystalline solar panel (2)	$230
Y-branch MC4 cable connectors, M/FF and F/MM	$10
15-foot 8-gauge MC4 solar extension cables	$36
Weatherproof solar cable entry gland	$19
Renogy 30-amp MC4 waterproof in-line fuse holder w/fuse	$15
30-amp circuit breaker fuse holder (3)	$40
150-amp circuit breaker fuse holder	$15
30-amp MPPT solar charge controller	$140
EPEVER MT50 solar remote LCD display	$30
AIMS power 1500-watt pure sine power inverter	$230
AIMS power inverter remote on/off switch	$25
Power strip with surge protector for 120-volt items	$15
6-gauge cable (10 feet)	$24
Wire crimp connectors, copper assortment	$25
Wire heat shrink tubing assortment	$10
¼-inch single stud ground junction block for 12-volt items	$10
12-volt rocker switch for kitchen lights and water pump (2)	$13
Wall-mount USB charging port	$20
12-way blade fuse block holder	$20
Total	**$1,745**

INTERIOR LIGHTING

12-volt LED lamps with built-in switch (4)	$60
Recessed 12-volt LED lights (6-pack)	$35
Total	**$95**

WATER SUPPLY

Camplux 5-liter propane water heater with showerhead	$140
33-gallon fresh water tank	$100
Shurflo 3.0 12-volt water pump	$60
Shurflo pre-pressurized accumulator	$34
Shurflo ½-inch twist-on pipe strainer	$9
½-inch PEX tubing (50 feet)	$35
½-inch PEX 90-degree fittings (6)	$18
½-inch PEX T-fittings (3)	$12
½-inch PEX shutoff valves (2)	$16
½-inch PEX crimp rings (20-pack)	$5
15 × 15-inch bar-style sink with faucet	$80
PVC sink drain pipe, fittings, P-trap	$20
Total	**$529**

GENERAL INTERIOR

Vinyl flooring (9 boxes/170 square feet)	$250
Futon sofa	$100
Area rug	$25
2-in-1 smoke alarm/carbon monoxide detector	$35
Heavy-duty magnet hooks (20-pack)	$25
Curtains	$30
Total	**$465**

KITCHEN

Reclaimed chest of drawers for kitchen cabinet	$80
Camp Chef propane oven	$175
Coleman steel-belted 54-quart cooler	$110
Reclaimed tabletop with hardware	$10
Drawer latches	$10
Total	**$385**

BATHROOM

Decorative privacy window film	$17
5-gallon bucket	$5
Toilet seat	$10
Curtain and curtain frame for outdoor shower	$20
Total	**$52**

BEDROOM

Queen mattress	$350
Materials for custom drawer under bed	$50
Total	**$400**

CLIMATE CONTROL

Cubic Mini Grizzly wood stove	$650
36-inch-long, 3-inch-diameter stove pipe, UL-103 approved (2)	$75
Dektite round high temp silicone pipe flashing (3 to 6¼ inches)	$33
3-inch universal stove pipe vent cap	$43
LG 8,000 Btu portable air conditioner	$275
Total	**$1,076**

DEMOLITION TOOLS

4½-inch angle grinder	$40
4½-inch, 1mm cut-off discs (10-pack)	$20
Wire brush attachment	$20
Crowbar	$15
Total	**$95**

PERSONAL PROTECTIVE EQUIPMENT

Safety glasses	$10
Gloves (two pairs)	$20
Rubber gloves (50-count box)	$10
Dust masks	$10
Ear protection	$10
Total	**$60**

RUST TREATMENT

POR-15 permanent rust preventative kit	$22

PAINT AND PREP MATERIALS

4 gallons industrial enamel paint	$180
3 gallons white elastomeric roof coating	$80
1 gallon black Rustoleum paint for bumpers/wheels/etc.	$50
1 quart white Rustoleum paint for mirrors and miscellaneous trim	$25
Brushes and rollers	$50
Sandpaper and scuff pads	$30
Painters' tape and paper	$25
Total	**$440**

EXTERIOR MATERIALS

Bicycle fork mounts (pair)	$40
Rear deck steel piping and flanges	$50
Rear decking boards	$24
Total	**$114**

CONSTRUCTION TOOLS

Cordless drill	$120
Spare drill batteries (2)	$100
Drill and screw bits assortment	$20
4-inch metal hole saw and pilot bit	$35
Jigsaw with blades	$50
Circular saw (used)	$20
Miter saw (used)	$30
Contractors' square	$10
Measuring tape	$10
SharkBite PEX tube crimp tool with go/no go gauge	$50
Caulking gun	$10
Knee pads	$20
Total	**$475**

CONSTRUCTION MATERIALS

2×3 framing boards (20)	$100
¾-inch plywood panels for bed frame (2)	$50
½-inch plywood subfloor panels (5)	$120
½-inch FOAMULAR insulation panels (5)	$180
2-inch FOAMULAR insulation panels (2)	$55
Reflective insulation roll for water tank (50 square feet)	$24
1×4 common boards for trim (10)	$95
1×10 common boards for shelving (2)	$24
4 × 8 sheets of white wall paneling (3)	$30
Locally milled lumber for interior walls	$100
1 quart wood stain	$10
1 quart polyurethane	$10
Waterproof caulk	$8
Heavy-duty, all-purpose adhesive	$12
Total	**$818**

CONSTRUCTION HARDWARE

½-inch self-tapping screws, metal to metal	$10
1-inch self-tapping screws, metal to metal	$10
2½-inch self-tapping screws, wood to metal	$12
1¼-inch wood screws	$8
2¼-inch wood screws	$10
L brackets (12)	$15
Total	**$65**

Total cost for the Book Bus build **$11,311**

RESOURCES

BLUE RIDGE CONVERSIONS

www.blueridgeconversions.org
A family business specializing in high-quality skoolie design and creation

BUS LIFE ADVENTURE

www.buslifeadventure.com
A great resource for conversion tips and highlighted skoolie builds

COLORADO CUSTOM COACHWORKS

www.coloradocustomcoachworks.com
Professional conversions, as well as assistance for the DIYer

NAVIGATION NOWHERE

https://navigationnowhere.com
A wealth of information and links to gear for all areas of the skoolie conversion process

SKOOLIE.NET COMMUNITY FORUMS

www.skoolie.net
The school bus conversion network

TINY LIFE SUPPLY

https://tinylifesupply.com
A hub for gear fit for a skoolie or any other tiny dwelling

METRIC Conversions

TO CONVERT	TO	MULTIPLY
inches	millimeters	inches by 25.4
inches	centimeters	inches by 2.54
inches	meters	inches by 0.0254
feet	meters	feet by 0.3048
yards	meters	yards by 0.9144

US (INCHES)	METRIC (CENTIMETERS)	US	METRIC
1	2.54	⅛ inch	3.2 mm
2	5.08	¼ inch	6.35 mm
3	7.62	⅜ inch	9.5 mm
4	10.16	½ inch	1.27 cm
5	12.70	⅝ inch	1.59 cm
6	15.24	¾ inch	1.91 cm
7	17.78	⅞ inch	2.22 cm
8	20.32	1 inch	2.54 cm
9	22.86		
10	25.40		
11	27.94		
12	30.48		

INDEX